JOHN KEATS

JOHN KEATS

from a pen and ink drawing of 1816 by BENJAMIN ROBERT HAYDON,
by courtesy of the National Portrait Gallery, London

WW

JOHN KEATS

Kelvin Everest

Northcote House
in association with the
British Council

First published in 2002 by Northcote House Publishers Ltd, Horndon, Tavistock, Devon, PL19 9NQ, United Kingdom.
Tel: +44 (0) 1822 810066 Fax: +44 (0) 1822 810034.

British Library Cataloguing-in-Publication Data
A catalogue record for this book is available from the British Library

ISBN 0-7463-0808-6 (Hbk)
     0-7463-0807-8 (Pbk)

Typeset by PDQ Typesetting, Newcastle-under-Lyme
Printed and bound in the United Kingdom
Bell & Bain Ltd., Glasgow

Contents

Acknowledgements

This book attempts to explain the reasons why Keats is a great writer. Its deepest debt is to those teachers, colleagues, and friends who have helped me to appreciate good poetry and its importance. I am pleased to acknowledge the influence and example of my English teacher at East Barnet Grammar School, Mr E. J. Ward; the marvellous teachers I encountered as an undergraduate at Reading University, especially Lionel Kelly, Christopher Salvesen, the late John Goode, the late D. J. Gordon, and the late Geoffrey Matthews (and also Christopher and Geoffrey as joint supervisors of my doctoral thesis); my fellow research student the late Celia Kendall; Gavin Edwards in our time together as colleagues at St David's University College, Lampeter; and Rick Rylance, Martin Stannard, Bill Myers, and Sandy Cunningham, who were colleagues at Leicester University. The English Department at Liverpool has provided a wonderfully stimulating and intellectually committed environment over the past ten years. I am very grateful to Sophie Everest, who helped to check pages, and produced the index. My greatest debt of all, however, is to Faith Everest. She is the reader I have tried always to bear in mind.

Biographical Outline

1795   John Keats born 31 October (according to baptismal entry), in London.

1797   Keats's brother George born 28 February.

1799   Keats's brother Tom born 18 November.

1801   Keats's brother Edward born (dies the following year).

1802   Keats family move to Swan and Hoop Inn and Livery Stables, Moorfields; Keats's maternal grandfather John Jennings has owned the leasehold since 1774, and installs Keats's father as manager.

1803   Keats's sister Fanny born 3 June. From August, Keats attends Clarke's School in Enfield with his brother George (joined later by Tom). Friendship with Charles Cowden Clarke.

1804   Keats's father is killed in a fall from his horse, 16 April. His mother quickly remarries William Rawlings, 27 June. Keats moves with his brothers and sister to live with his maternal grandparents, John and Alice Jennings, at Ponder's End.

1805   John Jennings dies, 8 March; Keats children move with Alice Jennings to Edmonton.

1810   Keats's mother dies in March from tuberculosis. In July Alice Jennings appoints two guardians for her grand-children, John Nowland Sandell and Richard Abbey (after Sandell's death in 1816 Abbey is sole guardian). Keats leaves Clarke's School in the summer and is apprenticed to the surgeon and apothecary Thomas Hammond in Edmonton.

1814   Keats begins to write verse probably in this year. His grandmother Alice Jennings dies in December, leaving Keats the beneficiary of various trust funds. He seems to have remained ignorant of some of these; the principal sum is administered by Abbey, who frequently disagrees with Keats about its use and obstructs access. Keats's sister Fanny lives with the Abbeys from this period.

1815 Comes under the poetic and political influence of Leigh Hunt. Writes sonnets, epistles, and exercises in a variety of lyric forms. Keats enters Guy's Hospital as a medical student in October, and does well. Living with other students in Southwark.

1816 Keats's first published poem, 'O Solitude', published in Hunt's *Examiner*, 5 May. Meets William Haslam and Joseph Severn, two of his most faithful friends, in the spring. Passes medical examinations in July and is eligible to practise as a physician. In August visits Margate with Tom, and moves in with his brothers in September at lodgings in Dean Street, Southwark. Keats's literary acquaintance widens significantly; he meets Hunt, Benjamin Robert Haydon, John Hamilton Reynolds. Writes 'On First Looking into Chapman's Homer' in October. Keats is listed as a certified apothecary in December, but he renounces his medical career to concentrate on a poetic vocation. Moves with his brothers to lodgings in Cheapside in November. In December Hunt's 'Young Poets' article in the *Examiner* introduces Keats with Shelley and Reynolds as the new young generation in English poetry. Finishes 'I stood tip-toe...' and 'Sleep and Poetry' by end of year. Keats meets P. B. Shelley in December, and Haydon takes the famous life mask.

1817 In January and February Keats's literary circle widens further; meets the Shelleys, Godwin, William Hazlitt. His first volume, *Poems*, published by C. & J. Ollier in March. Meets John Taylor, who expresses interest in publishing Keats. Through Taylor Keats meets Richard Woodhouse. By end of March has moved with his brothers to Well Walk in Hampstead. April–November, working on *Endymion*. Meets Charles Wentworth Dilke, James Rice, and Benjamin Bailey around this time. Keats visits the Isle of Wight in April, goes to Canterbury in May, and meets Isabella Jones in Hastings. Returns to Hampstead in June. Meets Charles Brown in late summer. Stays with Benjamin Bailey in Oxford, September–October. Hunt's influence is at its height, but Keats is reading Shakespeare and Milton intensively, and Hunt's dominance begins to wane. In October the Tory *Blackwood's Edinburgh Magazine* attacks the 'Cockney School' associated with Hunt. Finishes *Endymion* at Burford Bridge in early December. Long sequence of major letters begins around this time, with 'Adam's Dream' letter to Bailey. Meets Wordsworth in December; attends the 'immortal dinner' with Haydon, Lamb, and Wordsworth, 28 December. Late December, 'Negative Capability' letter to his brothers.

1818   January, Keats's brother Tom is spitting blood. 'Axioms of Poetry' letter to Taylor in February. Writes 'Epistle to Reynolds' in March. Keats stays with Tom in Teignmouth, March–April. Writes Preface to *Endymion*, and after this is rejected writes second version. *Endymion* published in April by Taylor & Hessey. Finishes writing *Isabella; or, The Pot of Basil*. Letter to Reynolds on life as a 'Large Mansion of Many Apartments', 3 May. George Keats marries Georgiana Wylie, end of May; they emigrate to America, and Keats and Charles Brown accompany them to Liverpool end June, and then begin a walking tour of the Lake District and Scotland. Keats breaks off his tour in August having fallen ill with a severe cold and bad sore throat; returns to Hampstead by 18 August to find Tom gravely ill. Savage critical attacks on Keats appear in September in the *Quarterly Review*, *Blackwood's*, and the *British Critic*. Keats starts work on *Hyperion* in September, and nurses Tom. He meets Isabella Jones again in October. Writes 'Chameleon Poet' letter to Woodhouse in October. Meets the 18-year-old Fanny Brawne in November. Tom dies 1 December. Keats moves into Wentworth Place in Hampstead (now Keats House) with Brown. On Christmas Day Keats comes to an 'understanding' with Fanny Brawne.

1819   January, Keats visits Chichester, and Bedhampton. Writes *The Eve of St Agnes*. February, attempts, but abandons, a sequel, 'The Eve of St Mark'. Writes 'Continual Allegory' letter to his brothers in February. Fanny moves in with her mother next door to Keats in Wentworth Place, 3 April. Keats gives up *Hyperion* in April. 11 April, walk on Hampstead Heath with Coleridge. April–May, experimenting in various sonnet and lyric forms; writes 'La Belle Dame sans Merci', 'Ode to a Nightingale', 'Ode on a Grecian Urn', 'Ode on Melancholy'. Journal-letter February–May to his brothers includes passage on life as a 'Vale of Soul-Making'. May, has serious family and money worries; considers giving up poetry. June–September, visits Shanklin, Isle of Wight, with a visit to Winchester with Brown in August; working on *Otho the Great*, *Lamia*, *The Fall of Hyperion*. Writes 'To Autumn', 19 September. Returns to London in October after abandoning *The Fall of Hyperion*. Takes lodgings in Westminster, in effort to 'wean' himself from Fanny; returns to Wentworth Place, next door to the Brawnes, in November. Working on *King Stephen*, *The Cap and Bells*, last attempt to continue with *Fall of Hyperion*. Unwell by December; engaged to Fanny.

1820   George Keats returns to London, with financial problems. *Otho the Great* rejected by Covent Garden. After George's departure, Keats has severe haemorrhage on 3 February. Offers to break off his engagement to Fanny; she refuses. Keats's health is in serious rapid decline, February–May. Moves to Kentish Town in May, and then in June to Hunt's house. July, Keats's third and final volume, *Lamia, Isabella, The Eve of St Agnes, and Other Poems* (including the Odes, and *Hyperion*) published by Taylor & Hessey. 5 July, ordered to Italy for his health. In August Shelley invites Keats to stay with him in Italy; he declines. Abbey refuses to advance funds. Keats quarrels with Hunt and moves in with the Brawnes. He makes an informal will. Sails for Italy in September, accompanied by Severn. Delayed by storms and calms, and on arrival at Naples in October the ship is held in quarantine. Keats reaches Rome 15 November, taking lodgings in the Piazza di Spagnia. Has final relapse on 10 December.

1821   Keats dies at 11.00 p.m. on 23 February. Buried in the Protestant Cemetery in Rome on 26 February.

Abbreviation and References

Quotations of Keats's poems are taken from *John Keats: The Complete Poems*, ed. John Barnard, 3rd edn. (Harmondsworth: Penguin, 1988).

The following abbreviation is used in the text:

L.   *The Letters of John Keats*, ed. Hyder E. Rollins, 2 vols. (Cambridge, Mass.: Harvard University Press, 1958)

1

Why Read Keats?

A powerful modern image of Keats represents him as the very incarnation of the conventionally 'poetic'. His poetry is often taken to embody a desire to escape from the harsh and unforgiving real world, into an imaginary realm of unchanging perfection and ceaseless pleasure. This is a common view amongst readers new to Keats, and indeed new to poetry, and it is deeply engrained in contemporary popular culture. It derives, ultimately, from a more meditated and informed school of thought, including many academic readers, which sees Keats as a central representative of the Romantic movement, and which thinks of that movement as an abdication of moral and intellectual responsibility. The argument is that the English Romantic movement in poetry of the early nineteenth century was a reaction against the changes wrought to the forms of personal and social life, and to the environment, by industrialization and its accompanying economic and political upheavals. The Romantic seeks refuge from these pressing realities, in the self, in nature, the imagination, the past; anything is preferable to direct engagement with the real circumstances and issues of contemporary life, riven as that life was by deep domestic social conflict, and by international war. Keats above all the major English Romantics can seem to lend himself to this kind of reading, for it cannot be denied that the bulk of his poetry offers no obvious direct reflection of, or commentary upon, the crises of his times.

In fact Keats can appear at first sight to offer no commentary on anything at all. One of the biggest difficulties for new readers of Keats is to come to an understanding of what his poetry is actually *about*. Its declared themes – beauty, love, erotic experience, the fleetingness of experience, and the power of art to take experience out of time – are not usually presented in a context of sustained argument, nor are they presented in relationship with Keats's own ordinary social experience. His handling of such themes is, on the contrary, strikingly abstract, which compounds the effect of their inherent abstraction, and this can make his poetry seem preoccupied principally with the desire to embody the ideal, to *become* the ideal, and thus to make the poetry itself the very form of escape for which the poet seems to yearn.

This image of Keats, as a writer whose work is concerned with poetry as a form of escape from reality, is certainly a misreading, but it is a misreading that does nevertheless respond to qualities that are present in his work. Recent readings of Keats in his historical context, which seek in various ways to read his poetry as a form of political or historical engagement, have been numerous and influential, and most critics would now agree that Keats knew all about his contemporary world, and that his poetry is a form of representation of that world. The obliquely indirect and relatively abstracted nature of this representation still, however, poses a real critical problem. This book attempts to develop a way of reading Keats that gives proper countenance to his rootedness in time and history. But Keats's qualities as a poet can be obscured and distorted by a determinedly historical reading, quite as much as by an exclusive emphasis on his abstractness and the intensity of his engagement with imaginative experience. Keats was interested in time, history, reality; it is where he lived. But it is also clear that he was interested in other kinds of existence, and that his poetry is deeply engaged with the problem of what it might mean to live out of time.

Keats can be thought of as an escapist, a poet of pure imagination. He can quite oppositely be thought of as a poet very much of his own times, producing a poetry whose contemporary reference has been long obscured. Both interpretations naturally owe a great deal to the history of his posthumous reputation, in which Keats has come to play an important role in cultural debate about the place of poetry in the modern world. As with other great poets, the nature of his artistic achievement finds redefinition with the changing emphases of the critical community. In the Victorian period, when there was a pressure to think of idealism as unlikely to flourish in the real world, Keats's poetry, like that of his contemporary and acquaintance Percy Bysshe Shelley, was considered to be wholly committed to the life of the imagination, as distinct from the reason and from social responsibilities. In recent times, when academic criticism in Western Europe and the United States has come to lay great stress on the inescapable influence of historical and social contexts, Keats has been newly read as a poet of political commitment, in the liberal cause, whose straightforward or oblique social and political reference has been seriously misrecognized by preceding generations of readers. In short, interpretations of Keats himself, and of his work, have since his death served strikingly to embody larger patterns of emphasis and outlook in the literary-critical community. He now as a consequence has a cultural meaning that has become closely bound up with judgements of his actual poetry. It is for this reason impossible to think about Keats's achievement without consideration of his life story, and its many retellings. His life has effectively become one of his most important works of art. His case can serve as the prime instance of the artist who embraces his art as a self-sufficient and autonomous realm; or, conversely, it can be used to prove the impossibility of escape from determining historical conditions. Keats's meaning for his readers has altered with the altering larger debates around these questions.

Keats's achievement as a poet has, however, a further special resonance and meaning for modern readers. His example affirms that English poetry is an art form for the people as a whole, and not the preserve of a privileged elite. In Keats's poetry the English poetic tradition is claimed for a fundamentally democratic future, in which high aesthetic experience is the possession of a wider and socially inclusive readership. And this claim is made, pre-eminently, by Keats as a practitioner; he recognized the power and vitality of poetry, but also, with determined and courageous self-belief, he recognized his own right to take a place amongst the English poets.

Keats's right to be a poet was hardly obvious to his contemporaries, and indeed, as we shall see, it was publicly contested in the most savage fashion by reviewers of his published work. He was not privileged in his birth and

3

upbringing. He did not have a classical education. His writings and biography suggest that he was not a practising Christian, and indeed the values he lived by cannot be referred to any of the great belief-systems. When he approaches subjects that are associated with traditions of formal thinking, he tends to represent himself, self-consciously, as inexperienced and un-tutored. It has often been said that he came to the English poetic tradition, as he came to English society, as something of an outsider, and that he experienced both in the role of a looker-on, excluded by his circumstances from active and direct participa-tion. It is not always very clear from Keats's own attitudes, as recorded in his letters, and in the many recollections and accounts of him that have survived, whether or not he himself shared this feeling of being excluded. Critics have often pointed to the way that his poetry articulates a sense of straining for possession of some idealized object or condition that stays out of reach, or that can be grasped only fleetingly. But this is hardly unique to Keats, and his articulations of such striving need always to be weighed and judged in the full complexity of their poetic context. Nevertheless, to some of his contemporaries, such as Lord Byron, Keats did seem in his poetic ambitions to be trying for entry into a cultural domain that was not properly his. This aspect of the cultural reception of Keats seems to have a particular connection with the question of gender; the con-straints of his social status, with the limits it placed on what he could realistically hope to do and be in the real world of Regency London, mirror in some respects the limits experienced by women at that time. This has a particularly interesting inflection in contemporary attitudes to the sometimes frank eroticism of Keats's poetry, which seems to have provoked what one critic has aptly termed a 'socio-sexual revulsion' in some of his male readers who considered themselves Keats's social superiors.[1] It is as if the offence of a socially upstart pretension to poetic ambition was made doubly worse when it presumed to take sex as a subject.

This is a complicated area, and it is made more so by the awkward matter of Keats's own attitudes to women. He seems to have been more than unusually uncertain about his feelings towards women, whether as the objects of sexual desire, or as people. As he himself put it in a letter, 'I have not a right feeling

towards women' (*L.* i. 341). His awkwardness and embarrassment clearly owed a lot to his height; he was barely five feet tall,
and he refers often, directly or indirectly, to his lack of physical
stature, and to the self-consciousness this brought to his manner
with women. But there is also a difficulty in reconciling his
idealized image of women – idealized both as a 'pure Goddess'
and as the object of sexual desire and fantasy – with the reality
of his actual relationships and contacts. It is in this context very
striking that Keats consistently thinks of idealized objects of all
kinds in his poetry in the feminine, as, for example, in the
famous opening line of the 'Ode on a Grecian Urn'. The
different but related gender issues that are raised in Keats's
work make for a very interesting intersection with present-day
interest in the significance of gender, both in the formation of
human cultural identities and their representation in art, and in
the strong commitment in our own critical culture to explore
gendered ways of writing and reading.

These various ways of viewing Keats, with their implication
that he was unfitted for poetry, or that his poetry is somehow
flawed by the consequences of who he was, and when and
where he lived, are, of course, in significant ways a part of his
myth. But these images of Keats also now form part of his
modern importance, for they serve to identify his career with the
aspirations of today's real readership for poetry, which is diverse
in social and cultural background, and which finds itself coming
to poetry, often, with the sense of being disequipped for
enjoyment of serious poetry by a remoteness or exclusion from
the cultural context in which it was written, and to which it can
seem to speak. It is not simply that Keats's lack of a conventional
classical education aligns him with the great majority of today's
readers, although that is a profoundly important and far-
reaching circumstance. But, more fundamentally, his struggle
to make the received poetic tradition his own living possession
offers a model for fresh generations of readers, even in their
struggle to read Keats himself. There is also a repeating pattern
in Keats's poetic development, in which his own resources and
capacities are stimulated and released by an internalizing of the
resources of the tradition, its forms, styles, conventions, its
language, in a process of assimilative imitation. Keats grows into a
distinctive poetic identity of his own by successively inhabiting

the languages and styles of his poetic exemplars. His entire career may be characterized as a series of attempts to find a voice of his own by learning to speak the language of his most powerful poetic models; and in each case, perhaps with the exception of the great Spring Odes of 1819, the attempt ends just as Keats's own voice emerges, hesitantly and distinctively, to find itself speaking in a newly grown register, conscious above all of its own fresh emergence. It is a poetry that embodies the experience of growing into participation in a tradition, and its achievement becomes a form of fresh life for that tradition. It is the supreme model of the means by which poetry itself survives.

Keats's first important poem, the sonnet 'On First Looking into Chapman's Homer', written in October 1816 when he was still only 20, embodies these issues as its subject matter, with a startling prescience:

> Much have I travelled in the realms of gold,
>   And many goodly states and kingdoms seen;
>   Round many western islands have I been
> Which bards in fealty to Apollo hold.
> Oft of one wide expanse had I been told
>   That deep-browed Homer ruled as his demesne;
>   Yet did I never breathe its pure serene
> Till I heard Chapman speak out loud and bold:
> Then felt I like some watcher of the skies
>   When a new planet swims into his ken;
> Or like stout Cortez when with eagle eyes
>   He stared at the Pacific – and all his men
> Looked at each other with a wild surmise –
>   Silent, upon a peak in Darien.

This is a poem about poetry. The young Keats, who could not read Greek, celebrates his discovery of Homer in a sonnet that simultaneously celebrates its own poetic promise and precocity. The sense of wondering realization is focused primarily on a sudden grasping of literary relations in the West European tradition. As Keats reads Chapman's Elizabethan translation, the Homeric epic that he has known through allusion and influence takes on an affective reality as a reading experience, like a planet whose gravitational influence has been remarked before its existence is confirmed by direct observation.

This feeling of vast interlocking orbital systems, in which poets move as spheres of influence, underlies the sonnet's great brilliance of metaphorical play and development. The poem begins with the image of reading as a process of geographical discovery, implicitly based to the west of the region 'ruled' by Homer; that is to say, the poet's direct literary experience has been of Britain and perhaps of those regions immediately to the east (Keats knew French from his schooldays), and the literary discovery he now announces has taken him much further eastwards towards Greece, into regions known hitherto only by repute. The literary tenor of this metaphor is always in view: in the obvious references of the fourth line (Apollo was, of course, the Greek god of poetry), and less directly in the suggestivity of 'realms of gold' in line 1, which at once evokes a generalized imaginative world, and hints at the gilded pages of old books. The journey is conceived in spatial terms, with the European literary tradition thought of as existing as in a map of areas with fixed relations and centres of achievement, which Keats has visited in his reading. The metaphor suggests the manner of popular travel narratives (which Keats, like his contemporaries, read as we consume, say, crime fiction today). This suggestion of a travel narrative is heightened by the suggestion in the diction of a journey not just outwards but back in time, as if the places visited are not only far away but long ago; at first just rather long ago, as in the old-fashioned 'goodly' of line 2, but then receding to an almost fabulous feudal past, in 'fealty' and 'demesne', to give the Homeric achievement a kind of immemorial authority and culturally remote grandeur.

The poem's opening metaphor thus progresses towards a culminating image of Chapman's Homeric translation as the different atmosphere of a new place, perhaps long anticipated but still strikingly foreign in the actual breathing in: 'Yet did I never breathe its [i.e. the 'wide expanse' ruled by Homer] pure serene/Till I heard Chapman speak out loud and bold'. These lines also constitute a kind of culminating initial resting place, for the reader, in a different sense, as they can sound awkward, and technically unpractised. The poem's first eight lines have what might be considered a somewhat forced overliterary and factitious quality (Keats, we know, had not read all that impressively much more than the next man, and he had experienced actual travel hardly at all) and there is also an uncomfortable suspicion that the word order gets pulled out of shape by the formal demands of the sonnet, and that the rhyme words seem disconcerting, and with a tendency to change the direction of the unfolding sense. The 'loud and bold' way that Chapman speaks out particularly embodies these limiting features. It will be helpful to return to these aspects, because they can introduce us to some large questions about Keats's methods, attractions, and limits as a poet.

The sonnet moves to a different register in line 9, observing as it does with deft understatement the conventionally proper 'turn' in mood and argument of a Petrarchan sonnet. The Petrarchan form is generally considered something of a challenge in English because its rhyme scheme, which is repeated in the first and second quatrains (i.e. lines 1–4, and 5–8), is harder to meet in English than it is in Italian (because of the differing grammars), and harder to meet in this sonnet form than in the Shakespearian form, which uses three differently rhyming quatrains. The relative assurance with which Keats meets these formal demands is extraordinary, but not more so than the thickening density of implication and imaginative connectedness that now breeds in his development of the opening metaphor. For the geographical metaphor is, so to speak, projected from a regional to a global scale. The first direct experience of a literary masterpiece, an experience hitherto only guessed at on the basis of its presence in known texts, is not now likened simply to the arrival in a new place, but to the discovery of a new world in the literal sense. The reference of the metaphor is astronomical, and the idea of gravitational influence, and of the literary tradition suddenly comprehended as a system, now charges the feeling of wonder in discovery with a deeper excitement, as of a daring hypothesis spectacularly confirmed. The sense of a startling and momentous coming into focus of grand truths is exactly given in the epithet *swims*, which combines the effect of a compressed development to precise focalization with the dizzying and floorless feel of a transformative revelation.

This shift in the register of the metaphor gives Keats's sonnet a further dimension of affective power, and under its impetus the final four lines open into a further resonating development.

8

The image is of the *conquistador* Cortez, confronted with a vision of the Pacific after crossing the narrow isthmus of Darien, from its eastern to its western seaboard. His 'eagle eyes' stare, while his men are overtaken by a sudden shared 'wild surmise'. This wild surmise has, understandably, found many interpretations. But one that fits well with the sonnet's sequence of thought is that this is the moment when the explorers realize that the hypothesis that has prompted their journey in the first place, the hypothesis that the earth is a globe, and that therefore a journey westwards from Western Europe will arrive at the 'East' Indies, is about after all to be confirmed. 'After all', because landfall on the previously unknown American continent will at first have appeared as a disappointment; but the revelation of a further, vast ocean opens the possibility that, once traversed, the 'East' Indies will indeed be reached, and the earth will be confirmed as a globe. The moment thus implicitly echoes the previous image, because this too is the moment of discovery of a new planet, of the Earth *as* a planet. The logic of the poem's development circles round in its conclusion to encompass the full latent implication of an ambition to extend the map of one's literary experience. A map of that sort has no definable limits, but will, rather, sooner or later propose larger and still larger questions, which remove the understanding to an entirely different scale.

The closing 'wild surmise' also concentrates the sonnet's self-consciousness, its quality of dramatizing a process of self-discovery that gives a further dimension to the implications of the literary tenor of the poem's metaphors. The very imaginative energy that drives the poem forward proposes its poet as a new force within the gravitational field in which Homer's influence is exerted. The 'eagle eyes' of Cortez anticipate Keats's own repeated image of the poet as an eagle, and the 'wild surmise' of his men projects Keats's excited realization of the potential scale of his own talent. We did, however, note earlier that the sonnet has its limitations. It is, after all, no more than a sonnet, and not for instance an epic. There is a literary register in the poem's diction and phrasing that intensifies the effects of its self-reflexivity; it is a poem about poetry, by a poet who seems to know little *but* poetry, so that the revelation of his own poetic talent has a certain circularity, which can even seem like pointlessness. Should it not be a poem about poetry about something else? The technical accomplishment is in this context also part of the limitation, suggesting formal facility and completeness as ends in themselves, rather than as a means to some expressive goal beyond merely the celebration of the skill of the celebration.

But this kind of stricture takes us back to the big questions about Keats's achievement. Is he limited by the limited range of his experience? Is his concern with beauty, with poetry, as ends in themselves, simply a straightforward reflection of the fact that his experience was mostly from books and art? He was not rich, not learned, not travelled. How experienced was he in love? In sex? Did his social class not place him outside the realm of possibility in which contemporaries like Byron and Shelley moved so easily? He was never more than very young (he had only just turned 25 when he died, and by then he had been gravely ill for a year), and his life, like his poetry, sometimes seems like a succession of wishful imaginary projections forward in time, anticipating a richness of experience and a process of gradual enrichening self-development that was destined never actually to happen. These kinds of question can take many forms. Some recent historicist discussions have dwelt in particular on the disabling, or at least the shapingly delimiting effects of Keats's social class and background, in an eerie repetition of the attacks made on him in his own lifetime.[2] Younger new readers are sometimes quick to lose patience with Keats's abstraction and his self-conscious interest in the claims of art, and to deem him irrelevant to the interests of a socially engaged and politically motivated outlook, confident to make its investments in the here and now.

It is impossible to avoid the central emphasis on art in Keats's poetry. He returns constantly to the question of art's relation to experience, and he therefore is constantly preoccupied with the status and value of his own commitments and achievements as a poet. That is to say, his own art is always under interrogation when it takes as its central recurring subject the claims of art. But it is important to realize that Keats's commitment to the imagination, and his interest in the ideal, are not an evasion or a mode of escape from 'reality' (however conceived) but a means of relationship with it. Art is not experience, but is not in pure

10

opposition to it either, because its materials are drawn from experience and its timeless values must always obtain in the real time of actual artists and actual audiences. It is these kinds of relationship that form the true central subjects of Keats's poetry. And the relationship between art and reality is also crucial in the formation and distinctive identity of Keats's highly singular poetic idiom. The language of his poetry is at a remove from received varieties of both spoken and poetic English, but this remove serves in Keats to produce a disconcerting linguistic vitality. His writing is stranger than it seems, and a close attention to its detailed workings leads us to a heightened consciousness of the strange powers of language itself.

There is another reason why it is a mistake to think of Keats as remote from ordinary modern concerns, whether we think of his style or his subject matter. His preoccupation with art is inflected particularly as a preoccupation with artistic development, and more specifically with his own development as a poet. This is easy to understand in a young writer who was unusually sensitive to his own growth as an intelligence and an artist, and for whom this question of his own maturation was given a sharp edge by the sense of his own mortality. Keats was a doctor by training and would have known the implications of his family history of early death from 'consumption' (tuberculosis) well before the onset of his own symptoms (which roughly coincided with his most productive year, from mid-1818). Nevertheless, a body of poetry that has a central thematic preoccupation with its own evolving identity *as* a body of poetry, and that constantly poses the abstract question of its own emerging quality and usefulness, might seem at best rather too inward-looking.

But one of the most extraordinary features of Keats's achievement is his use of this preoccupation with his own poetic development as a metaphorical vehicle for more inclusive concerns, which can touch any kind and any generation of reader. There are three principle areas in which the idea of poetic development in Keats can be understood to serve wider thematic purposes. There is, first, a broader literary context. Keats's concern with his own development tends to merge with a larger representation of the development of poetry, and specifically English poetry, within a tradition. His own development has, of course, a particular piquancy considered in this light, because it bears on the question of his own ultimate place within the still growing tradition (growing, that is to say, in virtue of his own new contribution to that tradition). We have already touched on the dependent nature of Keats's career, the manner in which each new project is initiated from within an effort to write in the manner of an established model. This discernible pattern in his work builds to an enunciation of a central paradox in the identity of any national literary corpus considered in a developmental light. How do we comprehend each successive stage in the development of a tradition as a moving on, which is not at the same time a leaving behind? What is the relationship, in literary terms, between identity as a constantly new form into which we move, and identity as a fixed and completed entity, sufficient to itself? This paradoxical problem in literary history – is the relation between Milton and Shakespeare one of evolutionary development from a lower to a higher form? – is one specific form for the still larger and more abstract question of identity in time.

This takes us into the second area that is at stake in Keats's concern with development: the development of the self, and the relation of the self as fixed in qualities and experience at a particular moment to the self as constantly evolving, constantly growing away from its known properties and attributes. There is often an autobiographical dimension that is implicit in Keats's concern with his own poetic development, in the sense that this development images the more widely shareable problems of his own growth not as a poet, but simply as a person. This takes us back to the fundamental concern with time and permanence in Keats, and his recurring attempt to place the relation of transient experience to fixed meanings and values. Where does the value of experience reside? In experiences that are inherently transient, and defined by the temporality of their existence? Or in forms of experience that can be abstracted from the passage of time and the physical flux of the material world, such as works of art, or dreams, or ideals? We can see that, in this light, to talk of Keats's poetry as uninterested in history is irrelevant, for these are questions that bear on the very nature of human existence in time, and that are therefore inextricably bound up with the question of the meaning and value of history.

History is the third area that is implicit in Keats's concern with the idea of development, for here too there is a paradoxical relation between identity and process. The assumption that history is inherently progressive, and that there is, or could be, a continual development towards improved forms for individual and social life, appears to hold out an attractive long-term prospect for humanity. But there is a serious difficulty in such an apparently optimistic assumption, in that it undermines the value of present and actually known experience and circumstances. This problem lies at the heart of Keats's most ambitious efforts as a poet, in the unfinished fragments of *Hyperion* and *The Fall of Hyperion*, and it is implicit in all of his important writing. It is what might be thought of as the social-historical level of those other concerns we have noted; the relation of the changing, growing self to present experience and identity, and the relation of the individual poetic achievement to the larger tradition, the achieved sequence, of great poetry.

The connection between process and identity, the temporal and the fixedly permanent, is a problem not least in the identity of the poem as a work of art. A poem unfolds, if not over a definite period of time, then at least in a notionally linear order; it consists of parts that are understood as standing in a specific sequence, and the reader must move through this sequence (and no other). In this sense any poem has, so to speak, a certain narrative content, even if it is a lyric that tells no story in the ordinary sense. Poems make their effects, at least in part, as a developing process. But, of course, they also exist in a static way, like a painting, and the reading of a poem can also look at a poem as if it were an object, rather than a process. Keats is very aware of these questions about how a poem exists and works, and one of his greatest achievements, the 'Ode on a Grecian Urn', is the classic embodiment of the questions at issue. But in a more general way this problem about how a poem exists, as an object or as a process, is another form that the Keatsian themes we have been considering can take. Indeed, the poems thereby themselves come formally to embody, or enact, Keats's interest in the relations between self and change, time and permanence, experience and art.

The account of Keats's life and work that follows is straightforwardly chronological, and its emphasis is primarily

13

on Keats's poetic development. But it should not be assumed that this emphasis implies that Keats's interest and importance are chiefly to be understood in aesthetic terms. As we have already seen, Keats's aesthetic concerns, and his practice, are bound up with larger questions. The basic purpose of this introductory chapter is to open up the poetry in its full range of implication and achievement. That achievement lies essentially in Keats's unflinching dedication to interrogate the purpose and final claims of art in relation to life. The story of his own life is then for us, as it was for him, inseparable from his achievement as a poet.

2

October 1795–October 1816: Early Poems

John Keats was born in London in October 1795. Amongst the many myths that came to surround this circumstance was the belief that he was born in a coaching inn, the Swan and Hoop at 24 The Pavement, Moorgate, and that his father, Thomas, was an 'ostler' in the inn. This supposed humble origin was to play its part in savage politically inspired attacks made on Keats by Tory reviewers during his lifetime, and it deeply coloured the nineteenth-century biographical tradition. It is difficult to translate the nuances of social class from those familiar to us today. But Keats's parents were not impoverished, and there was certainly money on his mother's side of the family. There is in fact no evidence that Keats was born at the Swan and Hoop. His first demonstrable connection with it was at the age of 7 in 1802, when his father was installed as manager of the inn by his father-in-law (Keats's maternal grandfather), who owned it together with neighbouring properties.

Keats had nothing approaching the privileges enjoyed, for example, by his slightly older contemporaries Shelley and Byron, who were both born into landed aristocratic families. Neither did he enjoy the kind of patronage that made a writer's life possible for William Wordsworth, or Samuel Taylor Coleridge. But it would be a mistake to think of Keats's family as 'working class'. His circumstances are in marked contrast with those of William Blake, for instance, who had no formal education other than a trade apprenticeship, and who had to work long and hard all his life as an engraver simply in order to support himself. Although Keats's financial affairs were tangled and obscure, he was not without means of his own.

The question of Keats's origins made for serious difficulty in the development of his reputation. The critical attacks launched against him by Tory Reviews in 1818, and that notoriously but very effectively attached to him the pejorative label of 'Cockney', were prompted in the main by Keats's association with the radical journalist and poet Leigh Hunt. These attacks played on the supposed obscurity of Keats's social background, and introduced a dimension in public discussion of Keats that was further confused by various statements made by his friends and acquaintances after his death. These were usually perfectly well intentioned, but many have exerted a disproportionate influence, and none more so than those by Leigh Hunt himself, who wrote in *Lord Byron and Some of his Contemporaries*, published in 1828, seven years after Keats's death, that

> Mr Keats's origin was of the humblest description; he was born October 29, 1796, at a livery-stables in Moorfields, of which his grandfather was the proprietor. I am very incurious, and did not know this till the other day. He never spoke of it, perhaps out of a personal soreness which the world had exasperated. After receiving the rudiments of a classical education at Mr Clarke's school at Enfield, he was bound apprentice to Mr Hammond, a surgeon, in Church-Street, Edmonton; and his enemies having made a jest even of this, he did not like to be reminded of it...[1]

Hunt clearly meant well, and the account he goes on to give is generous, perceptive, and foreseeing: Keats was 'as true a man of genius as these latter times have seen; one of those who are too genuine and too original to be properly appreciated at first, but whose time for applause will infallibly arrive'. It is also true that, throughout all the surviving records, Keats maintains a curiously absolute silence concerning both his mother and his father, which does suggest some strong unarticulated feelings concerning his family background. But Hunt's version of Keats's 'origin', mistaken as it is in almost every particular, helped to perpetuate various biographical fallacies that became part of Keats's myth. And this question has remained at the very heart of public discussion of Keats's career and achievement.

Little is known of Keats's father, described as a man of common sense and respectability, whom Keats resembled in a short, stocky build, and an attractively alert bearing. The family name appears to originate in Devon or Cornwall, and there is evidence that Thomas Keats may have come from Reading. His marriage on 9 October 1794, at St George's, Hanover Square, was apparently a rushed affair. The couple were young and there were no family witnesses. Frances Jennings, the poet's mother, was recalled as excitable and attractive, and there is much to suggest also a reckless impetuosity. Her father, John Jennings, was a man of property who purchased the leasehold of the Swan and Hoop in 1774, adding the next-door property in 1785. Keats's brother George was born in 1797, Thomas in 1799, and Edward in 1801 (but he died before the end of the following year). The only sister, Fanny, was born in 1803. George and Tom were to play a significant part in Keats's short, intense life, George in the role of hard-headed realist, while Tom enjoyed a special empathy with his poet brother.

In August 1803 Keats went to Clarke's School in Enfield. The headmaster was John Clarke, whose son Charles Cowden Clarke was an usher at the school. But Keats had barely begun his school life when his family was overtaken by catastrophe. On 16 April 1804, his father was killed in a fall from his horse. Keats's newly widowed mother almost immediately married one William Rawlings, on 27 June at St George's, Hanover Square. The startling haste of this remarriage has fuelled speculation that Rawlings was an adventurer interested in Frances Keats's inheritance of some £2,000. The couple took up residence in the Swan and Hoop, with Rawlings as manager.

Family relations now deteriorated badly, with consequences that cast a shadow over all Keats's subsequent experience. His grandfather John Jennings died on 8 March 1805, leaving a substantial estate that made generous provision for the various members of his family. As well as Keats himself, these included his widow, Alice, Keats's mother, brothers, and sister, and his uncle the naval officer Midgley Jennings and his family, and John Jennings's sister, Mary Sweetinburgh. But the terms of the will proved ambivalent and were challenged in Chancery by Keats's mother, thus complicating and delaying any actual payment, to her brother, herself, or Keats. The action ultimately failed completely following judgement by the Master of the Rolls on 29 July 1806. Frances parted from Rawlings around this time, and her whereabouts in the following three years are a mystery.

17

Keats's maternal grandmother, Alice Jennings, had after her husband's death lived in a rented house in Ponder's End north of London. Soon after her daughter's challenge to the will, the Keats children left their mother and stepfather at the Swan and Hoop and went to live with their grandmother in a new address in Church Street, Edmonton, near to Clarke's School. This arrangement apparently consolidated a serious split in the family, whereby Keats found himself caught up in bitter alienating enmity between his mother, his grandmother, and also his uncle Midgley, whose supposed military heroics Keats was said to have idolized as a boy. The situation perhaps goes some way to explain Keats's subsequent silence on the subject of his parents.

When Midgley died of a 'decline' (tuberculosis) on 21 November 1808, at 31 ominously young, Keats's mother, Frances, revived her original Bill of Complaint, but her failure to pursue it supports the possibility that she was reconciled with the family by the summer of 1809. Midgley's stock was divided equally between his widow and Alice Jennings. This meant that under the terms of his grandfather's will Keats could apply to Chancery at any time after his twenty-first birthday for a quarter share of the estate, about £800.

The period of his mother's reconciliation with the family coincided with a change of attitude by Keats at school. Charles Cowden Clarke became a firm friend of Keats, and his *Recollections of Writers* includes a vivid account of the young poet. Clarke remembered him as the 'favourite of all' for his 'high-mindedness, his utter unconsciousness of a mean motive, his placability, his generosity'.[2] He had from an early age a striking physical presence remarked by observers throughout his life. At school he was conspicuous for extremes of passion, with a determination and physical courage belying his small stature. Another close friend of Keats at school was Edward Holmes, the future biographer of Mozart, who remembered Keats in childhood as attached not to books but to 'all active exercises', with a special relish for fighting.[3] However, after January 1809 Keats surprised everyone with a resolve to 'carry off all the first prizes in literature'[4] – a determination in which he succeeded. Keats's education at Clarke's was probably better than at the typical public school of the day. He covered scientific

18

and practical subjects, Latin and French, and, although he never learnt Greek, he imbibed from such works as Lemprière's *Classical Dictionary* an 'intimacy with the Greek mythology'.[5] The school's liberal principles were especially significant. Keats's first acquaintance with Leigh Hunt's *Examiner* dates from this time, and it was at Clarke's that Keats's politically radical sympathies, and his youthful enthusiasm for Hunt, began to develop. Keats's schoolboy friends, and particularly Cowden Clarke, strongly influenced his early reading and literary tastes, notably for Spenser. Keats and Clarke seem, however, to have drifted out of contact after 1817.

Keats's new commitment to his studies in 1809 no doubt owed much to renewed intimacy with his mother, which also brought new responsibilities, as she was clearly unwell. Keats had already demonstrated a strong sense of family responsibility in his watchful solicitude for his little sister, Fanny, and his younger brothers, which would continue throughout his life. But all sense of domestic security was destroyed by the death of his mother in March 1810, like Midgley from a 'decline'. Keats, who had always been markedly protective of his mother, gave himself up to 'a long agony of grief', hiding under an alcove beneath a master's desk at school.[6] Keats's grandmother, Alice Jennings, now had a substantial estate to dispose of, having seen all other claimants die. On 30 July 1810 she executed a deed making the property over to John Nowland Sandell, a merchant, and Richard Abbey, a friend from her native village of Colne in Lancashire, to administer for her grandchildren. After Sandell's death in 1816, Abbey became sole guardian.

II

Keats left Clarke's School in the summer of 1810, and at 14 was apprenticed to the surgeon and apothecary Thomas Hammond, neighbour and doctor of the Jennings family. Keats moved in above his surgery at 7 Church Street, Edmonton. There seems no basis for the surmise of various biographers that Keats was forced into medical training, but the apprenticeship was expensive and began immediately to eat into the inheritance held in trust by Abbey. He made excellent progress, whilst his friendship with Cowden Clarke blossomed and his literary interests broadened and developed quickly. He kept up his school contacts and continued to receive informal tuition, completing a prose translation of the *Aeneid*. Some time probably in 1813 Keats quarrelled with Hammond and moved out, perhaps to live with his brothers in St Pancras. George had been removed from school early to work in Abbey's counting house as a clerk, where he would shortly be joined by Tom. Keats's great aunt Mary Sweetinburgh died in November 1813, and his grandmother Alice in December 1814. Keats told Richard Woodhouse that his early sonnet 'As from the darkening gloom a silver dove', as nearly Christian in sentiment as anything he wrote, was composed on her death. Fanny went to live with Abbey, who made it difficult for the brothers to visit, and discouraged correspondence. She remained with the Abbeys until her twenty-first birthday. Keats now had two sets of property in trust: £800 from John Jennings's will, and his share of the property held by Sandell and Abbey, which amounted to a quarter share in some £8,000. Keats never applied for the £800, and probably knew nothing of it. Although Abbey has often been blamed, he probably knew no more of it than Keats. William Walton, solicitor for Keats's mother and grandmother, certainly did know of it and should have informed Keats. George Keats was also ignorant of this money. On the death of Tom the surviving brothers' share was further augmented. This money could have made a very great difference to Keats, particularly as he struggled for funds in the last two years of his life.

According to Charles Brown, Keats did not think of writing verse until he had turned 18. His earliest known work, an 'Imitation of Spenser', dates probably from early 1814. This, like most of the poetry surviving from his student days, is markedly derivative. Obvious models for the early work include Byron, Hunt, and popular writers of the day such as Chatterton and Moore. But even the 'Imitation of Spenser' has a quality of self-reflection that foreshadows Keats's genius in working through literary models to an idiom entirely his own.

The immediate literary inspiration for Keats's 'Imitation of Spenser' comes, of course, from the Elizabethan poet Edmund Spenser, and in particular his long romance epic *The Faerie Queene*, which was to remain one of Keats's favourite works. Keats's 'Imitation' is on the face of it a slight and conventional exercise in the Spenserian stanza (nine lines rhyming *ababbcbcc,* written in iambic pentameter with an extra foot in the last line), but Keats published it in 1817 in his first volume, and in some respects the poem stands aptly at the very beginning of Keats's poetic career. The poem's four stanzas open with what seems like the continuation of an ongoing narrative: 'Now morning from her orient chamber came...'; but the lines that follow do no more than describe an island in a lake, a place that is conceived as a suitable setting for a story that does not itself get told. The nearest the poet comes is to lament an apparent inability to 'tell the wonders' of the isle, and to imagine that, were he able to tell the story, it would outdo some formidable literary models:

> Ah! could I tell the wonders of an isle
> That in that fairest lake had placèd been,
> I could e'en Dido of her grief beguile;
> Or rob from aged Lear his bitter teen.
>
> (ll.19–22)

The description of the lake, the island, and their surroundings luxuriates in the sensuous attractions of an imaginary natural setting; but the only thing that actually happens is the poem itself. We can discern in this early effort a number of characteristic features. The poem is intensely, indeed very self-consciously, *literary*. Its title announces this obviously enough, but the inward-looking effect of a poem that openly looks to emulate another poem, and that in a way chiefly exists in order to do that, is compounded by the combination of a narrative style with the absence of actual story. It is also compounded by the central image of reflection in the lines. The sky and surroundings of the lake are described as reflected in its waters, and particularly as these reflections merge with sights that are not merely reflected on the surface, but really existent beneath the surface:

> There the king-fisher saw his plumage bright
> Vying with fish of brilliant dye below;
> Whose silken fins, and golden scalès light
> Cast upward, through the waves, a ruby glow.
>
> (ll.10–14)

This blending of surface reflection with true depth points forward to pervasive qualities of Keats's mature poetry, where the reader is constantly challenged to distinguish between the poetry's self-reflexive concern with art, and its reach outwards to engage with the great themes of human experience. The teasing absence of a specific story in the 'Imitation of Spenser' is then aptly symbolic of the problem of the content of Keats's poetry. And when Keats claims in the poem that, were he able to tell the story of the island in the lake, then it would be more powerful than the stories of the *Aeneid*, or *King Lear*, this strengthens the effect of circularity and self-reference, by suggesting literature itself as the actual content of the literature Keats wishes he could produce. The 'Imitation of Spenser' also anticipates the major poetry in a different way. Its idealized imaginary representation of a perfected nature is given by the verse with a sensuous immediacy that returns us to the real experience of our senses. It is, as Keats will later say, a dream, but a dream of the truth, in which the place to which we escape from reality turns out to be a heightened re-encounter with that reality. Keats's poetic imagination is in this sense highly distinctive in resolutely avoiding any sense of transcendence. The ideal is a version of where we already are.

The non-transcendent idealism of Keats's poetic imagination has an important political significance, for it implies that happiness is to be found only through some form of direct experience. Our highest ideals are founded in our experience of the real world in which we live, so there is a moral imperative to do what may be done always to improve the real conditions of experience. In this sense Keats's poetic idealism is coherent with a meliorative rational radicalism, of the kind that found an influential exponent in Keats's time in the philosophical anarchism of William Godwin, and that also underpins the thought of the critic and essayist William Hazlitt, who had a considerable influence on Keats. There is, however, a paradoxical contrary implication in Keats's non-transcendent idealism, because it means that his conception of the ideal and the perfect is closely wedded to direct experience and its existing conditions. The better world that we can imagine, and towards which, in the best traditions of political radicalism, we may strive to move our own world, is not something we can have known through our senses, or have tested 'on our pulses'. And this implies a kind of fundamental conservatism of outlook, because of the high value attaching to the really existent conditions of our experience. In this light, any notion of change, poetic, personal, or social-historical, is likely to be attended by uncertainty and apprehension. To move towards the unknowable world of the future involves a renunciation of the truth of our established identity and its experiential context. In Keats's mature poetry we meet often with a greeting of change and flux as the inevitable and even the defining condition of pleasure, which nevertheless also strikes an elegiac note in conceding the necessity of relinquishing present identity and circumstance; for this is tantamount to relinquishing all that we have known of good as well as bad, pleasure as well as pain.

Although the 'Imitation of Spenser' is, of course, small scale in its ambitions and extremely modest in achievement, its qualities do indeed suggest a kind of prescience in Keats that rapidly takes on a subtle self-consciousness. In anticipating his own development he immediately turns such anticipation into a theme of, as it were a content for, the poetry that will make up the substance of the anticipated achievement.

His verse over the next eighteen months demonstrates a persistent preoccupation with the idea of his own literary vocation and destined fame. There is also a clear affinity with liberal political ideals and heroes. The sonnet 'Written on the Day that Mr Leigh Hunt left Prison' dates from February 1815, some eighteen months before Keats's first meeting with Hunt but explicitly acknowledging his influence. Like the 'Imitation of Spenser' this was published in Keats's *Poems* in 1817. It offers no substantial political commentary, but the mere fact of its support for Hunt, who as the poem says had been 'shut in prison' for 'showing truth to flattered state' (Hunt was released in 1815 after serving two years for libelling the Prince Regent in the *Examiner*), was sufficient publicly to mark Keats's political and cultural affiliations. Those affiliations are also clear in other early poems, as in the lines beginning 'Infatuate Britons', which celebrate the anniversary of the restoration of Charles the Second, and which pay tribute to the Whig heroes Sir Henry Vane, Lord William Russell, and Algernon Sidney. Such references demonstrate the nature of Keats's allegiances, as well as the fact of their existence; but such overt engagement with political ideas and personalities was not to be the norm in Keats's poetry. As his efforts in writing poetry evolved, through 1814 and 1815, and as they continued to develop after his entry

23

as a medical student at Guy's in October 1815 and into 1816, what is striking is the primarily literary cast of his subjects: an 'Ode to Apollo', the Greek god of poetry to whom Keats was memorably to return in *Hyperion*; sonnets on Byron and on Thomas Chatterton, the poet who had killed himself in poverty at the age of 17 in 1770. There are further Spenserian exercises, 'Specimen of an Induction to a Poem' and 'Calidore', which again exemplify the peculiarly Keatsian theme of consciously having no theme with which to fill out a poetic form.

By the middle of 1815 Keats had been introduced through his brother George to George Felton Mathew, an aspiring young poet and member of a poetical set consisting mainly of young ladies, including Mathew's own cousins. Keats wrote some thinly mannered verses to members of this group, typified by the lines 'To Some Ladies' in the tripping quatrains of Tom Moore. This set was soon outgrown, and Mathew was to prove ungenerous. But he stimulated Keats to new reading, in Fairfax's Tasso, for example, and helped to focus Keats's youthful sense of literary ambition.

Keats entered Guy's Hospital as a student, and followed a career implying some powerful patronage, as well as a genuine determination to qualify as a doctor. The distinguished surgeon Astley Cooper placed Keats under his own dresser, George Cooper, with whom he took lodgings close to the hospital at 28 St Thomas's Street in Southwark, with other medical students. The costs of this expensive new stage in his medical education further depleted the capital in Abbey's care, particularly after Keats was accepted as a dresser on 29 October, two days before his twentieth birthday. This was quick promotion and heralded a promising career.

The quality and seriousness of Keats's medical training, like his schooling, were for many years misleadingly downplayed or misrepresented in the biographical tradition. There is no doubt that Keats took his career as a medical student seriously, although retrospective accounts of his student days by his fellow students tended to play up to the Victorian image of Keats as the dreamer-poet. His student notebook survives (although it suggests an unmethodical approach), and the fact that he passed his exams, when plenty of his contemporaries did not, strongly implies that he was properly prepared and committed. As late as May 1819 Keats was still thinking seriously of escaping his problems by becoming a ship's surgeon.

Keats's medical training in fact represents a profoundly significant phase in his development. He will have encountered terrible human suffering with a directness that few modern readers are likely to have shared, and it is salutary always to keep this fact in mind when the nature of Keats's engagement with the real world is in question. As a 'dresser' he would have accompanied the senior doctors on their hospital rounds, and he assisted with operations and came to perform some himself. In the early years of the nineteenth century there was, of course, no effective anaesthetic, and no grasp of the significance of hygienic conditions in reducing the risk of infection; surgery in particular was an art in which speed was important, and mortality rates under treatment very high. Keats devoted five years of his short life to his medical training, and a great deal of his money, and after he had decided definitely to give it up in December 1816, soon after his twenty-first birthday, he continued to return to his medical experience in his poetry, and to worry at the relative usefulness to mankind of the callings of poet and doctor.

Keats's training as a doctor will also have left its mark in other ways. Through Astley Cooper at Guy's Keats would have come in contact with the work of John Abernethy and William Lawrence. These leading medical minds were engaged in a public controversy concerning fundamental problems about the very nature of 'life'. This controversy, driven by the great changes in scientific thinking that had been in train since the second half of the eighteenth century, focused especially on the question of how to define the property that distinguished living from non-living entities. Was this property something intrinsic to the matter of which a living body consisted? Or was it an external substance that conferred the property of 'life'? The argument was important and far-reaching in its implications. It raised serious religious questions about the nature and origins of human life. It also had a distinct political edge. Keats was born in 1795 when the revolutionary wars with France were already raging, and the Napoleonic Wars that convulsed all of Western Europe did not finally come to an end until Napoleon's final defeat at the battle of Waterloo in June 1815, when Keats was 19. In this period every kind of activity in England was perceived in a political light, because absolutely everything was pervaded by the shock of the French Revolution and its long aftermath. A controversy about the nature of life, which comprehended the possibility, for instance, of an entirely materialist explanation of the phenomenon of life itself, suggested the materialist doctrines of those eighteenth-century French thinkers whose influence was held at least partly to blame for the horrors of the Revolution itself. Keats may well himself have been acquainted with Abernethy and Lawrence; and it seems certain that he would have been caught up in the political arguments that pervaded the medical profession as they did every sphere of life at the time. It is, in short, impossible to sustain the notion of Keats's education and training as either limiting in themselves, or as irrelevant to the poetic career that followed. On the contrary, they inaugurated Keats's abiding preoccupation with the nature of the relationship between different kinds of life, and with the paradoxes and contradictions of personal and historical change.

Throughout the later months of 1815 Keats continued to write poems, exploring sonnet forms especially, but also giving expression to evidently quickening mental powers in work that shows the new influence of Wordsworth, such as the 'Epistle to George Felton Mathew' of November 1815. Keats's verse epistle, written in reply to Mathew's 'To a Poetical Friend', sketches the prospect of a poetic development that is overshadowed by distracting and uncongenial commitments (Mathew himself recorded that, when Keats wrote these lines, 'he was walking the hospitals'[7]):

> Too partial friend! fain would I follow thee
> Past each horizon of fine poesy;
> Fain would I echo back each pleasant note
> As o'er Sicilian seas, clear anthems float
> 'Mong the light skimming gondolas far parted,
> Just when the sun his farewell beam has darted –
> But 'tis impossible; far different cares
> Beckon me sternly from soft 'Lydian airs',
> And hold my faculties so long in thrall,
> That I am oft in doubt whether at all
> I shall again see Phoebus in the morning...

(ll.11–21)

This unwelcome curtailment even of a wholly imaginary forward projection of poetic development is to prove all too ominously characteristic in Keats. Here, in lines written soon after he had become a dresser at Guy's, it suggests a growing sense of misgiving about his commitment to a medical vocation. As his literary interests strengthened, and his poetic output started to build up – some thirty poems survive from the period up to September 1816, some of them reasonably substantial efforts – the pressure to make a difficult vocational decision must have increased sharply in Keats's mind.

'O Solitude!', a conventional Petrarchan sonnet also composed around this time, was to become Keats's first published poem when it appeared in the *Examiner* on 5 May 1816, thus strengthening Leigh Hunt's significance for Keats. Hunt agreed to print the poem without having met or presumably even heard of Keats.

Keats made friends easily. He was popular amongst his fellow students, and enjoyed a constantly widening circle of acquaintance. Amongst new friendships at this time, those with William Haslam and Joseph Severn, introduced through George Keats in the spring of 1816, were of particular importance. Haslam, who was about Keats's age and became a solicitor, was deeply attached to Keats and greatly admired his abilities. He remained a dependable friend and ally, often helping with financial problems. Severn, two years Keats's senior, was apprenticed as an engraver when they first became acquainted, but had already begun to work as a painter. Their friendship grew steadily, until in Keats's final months Severn's devoted care was to earn him a special place in English literary history.

Keats continued his medical studies, clearly to good effect. On 25 July 1816 he passed his exams to become a Licentiate of the Society of Apothecaries. This was a serious test of his medical knowledge, and made him eligible to practise as an apothecary, physician, and surgeon. Following this success Keats took a holiday from his studies and visited Margate with his brother Tom. They left in August, Keats continuing to write and completing three verse epistles in Margate, which further develop the themes of poetic vocation and, with a sharpening focus, the projection of his own poetic achievement. A verse epistle to his bother George composed at this time again attempts to imagine the substance of a poetic career, but now Keats's vision of such a career is much more noticeably driven by a real ambition, a newly focused sense that the poetic vocation is a means to a different and higher kind of life. After a passage that takes, in what is already a familiar pattern, a vision of what it will be like to write poetry as the actual thematic substance of the poem, Keats goes on explicitly to link his envisioned poetic career with the special reward of posthumous fame:

> These are the living pleasures of the bard:
> But richer far posterity's award.
> What does he murmur with his latest breath,
> While his proud eye looks through the film of death?
> 'What though I leave this dull, and earthly mould,
> Yet shall my spirit lofty converse hold
> With after times...'
>
> (ll.67–73)

And a few lines later this new scale of ambition is explicitly contrasted with the less troubling demands and rewards of a more practically useful social vocation:

> Ah, my dear friend and brother,
> Could I, at once, my mad ambition smother,
> For tasting joys like these, sure I should be
> Happier, and dearer to society.
> (ll.109–112)

Keats and his brother Tom returned from Margate to London in September, and took new lodgings at 8 Dean Street, Southwark with George, who had left Abbey's after quarrelling with a junior partner. Keats now faced a further period of study for his Membership of the Royal College of Surgeons.

3

October 1816–April 1818: 'I stood tip-toe...', 'Sleep and Poetry', *Endymion*

I

Immediately on his return to London Keats's life took a decisive turn as he was caught up in the excitement of powerful new literary friendships. By the middle of October he had been introduced by Cowden Clarke to his hero Leigh Hunt, after Clarke had showed Hunt some of his work. He expressed warm admiration, as did others such as Horace Smith, and a period of close intimacy with the Hunt circle began, matched by a newly dominant stylistic influence from Hunt in Keats's writing. Through Hunt Keats met the painter Benjamin Robert Haydon, already long launched on his picture *Christ's Entry into Jerusalem* and in the midst of public controversy over the authenticity of the Elgin Marbles. Keats was attracted to Haydon's artistic commitment and appetite for experience and argument, and Haydon, like many others at this time, was captivated by Keats's genial gusto and contagious sense of humour, and impressed by his passionate sense of poetic vocation. Another new friend, encountered through Haydon on 20 October, was John Hamilton Reynolds, a young writer with a promise that appeared to match Keats's own, and an easy-going quickness of wit that suited Keats's penchant for punning talk and artistic debate. The 'mad ambition' of Keats's epistle to his brother George appeared now less emptily fanciful, as the sense of a congenial literary community and audience began to gather substance.

The new intensity in Keats's literary life produced a burst of creativity. One evening in October Clarke introduced Keats to Chapman's translation of Homer, and after returning late to his lodgings he wrote the sonnet 'On First Looking into Chapman's Homer', which he contrived to have delivered to Clarke by 10 o'clock next morning. The astonishing achievement of this sonnet, with its confident formal assurance and metaphoric complexity, has already been discussed in the first chapter. As Hunt generously acknowledged, it 'completely announced the new poet taking possession'.[1]

Through November and December Keats's writing developed rapidly. He took on more directly the myth of his own personal and artistic growth, particularly in two long and ambitious poems, 'I stood tip-toe upon a little hill' and 'Sleep and Poetry'. These are experimental works, structurally unresolved and demonstrating Hunt's influence at its strongest, but most thoughtfully engaged with questions of literary history and Keats's place in it. Keats also began, with Hunt and others, to write poetry in timed competitions on agreed themes in prescribed forms, repeatedly demonstrating an exceptional facility in verse. George Felton Mathew had recently published 'To a Poetical Friend', on Keats, in the *European Magazine*, and on 1 December 1816 Hunt published the first of his 'Young Poets' articles in the *Examiner*, quoting the sonnet on Chapman's Homer in full, and representing Keats along with Shelley and Reynolds as the new generation in English poetry. Keats and Shelley met for the first time in mid-December. It was at this time that Haydon took his famous life mask of Keats.

In early December Keats was listed as a certified apothecary in the *London Medical Repository*, but the sense of poetic vocation was now clearly challenging Keats's commitment to his studies, and he decided to give up his career in medicine. Keats's deliberate decision to become a poet was the culmination of a period of intensifying literary experience, and productivity. His most favoured form at this time was undoubtedly the sonnet, in which by the end of 1816 he had become fluently practised, as the indulgence in timed sonnet-writing competitions graphi- cally demonstrates. The sonnet's demandingly concentrated patterns of rhyme suited Keats's liking for unconventional rhyme words, whilst providing a compact formal shaping that perhaps steadied Keats's uncertainty in the development of argument and a reasoned sequence of ideas. Keats's interest in the formal possibilities and limitations of the sonnet (and in related stanza forms such as the Spenserian) is a question to which we will return, as it is central in his development towards the achievement of the great odes of spring 1819. The two relatively long poems that really mark Keats's new confidence in verse at the end of 1816 are, in contrast, actually quite difficult to categorize in formal terms, and this formal singularity is an important aspect of their originality. On the face of it both 'Sleep and Poetry' and 'I stood tip-toe...' are very evidently written under the strong stylistic influence of Leigh Hunt. Take the opening lines of 'Sleep and Poetry':

> What is more gentle than a wind in summer?
> What is more soothing than the pretty hummer
> That stays one moment in an open flower,
> And buzzes cheerily from bower to bower?
> What is more tranquil than a musk-rose blowing
> In a green island, far from all men's knowing?

(ll. 1–6)

The couplets immediately suggest Hunt's versification in his *The Story of Rimini*, published in 1816; Keats wrote a sonnet in praise of Hunt's poem in March 1817, and it provides the epigraph to 'I stood tip-toe...'. Keats, like Hunt, very noticeably avoids the insistent end-stopping and balanced, antithetical manner perfected in the first part of the eighteenth century by Alexander Pope, and indeed the antipathy to Pope's manner and its influence is explicitly articulated later in the poem. This un-Pope-like verse texture remains characteristic throughout Keats's career, and there is a sense in which the conventional disparagement of Hunt's influence involves an element of perversity; Keats's distinctive strangeness and calculatedly mannered style would hardly have emerged as they did, after all, without the particular impetus of his enthusiasm for Hunt. But in this early manifestation the influence from Hunt is in part simply distractingly affected. The repeated use of so-called feminine metrical line endings, where the staple five-foot, ten-syllable iambic pentameter is continually supplemented by an extra unstressed syllable, gives a repetitive lightness, and combines in this effect with adverbs and adjectives ending weakly in '-y' (a very Huntian habit) and with a diction that seems actively to seek out weak terminal stresses of every kind, often emphasized by being in rhyme positions. These elements of style go with other qualities associated with Hunt, and especially with a kind of jaunty savouring of nature and seclusion that seems almost ludicrous in its unWordsworthian lightness and lack of a reflective dimension. This is the kind of thing that detractors of Hunt had in mind in aiming the pejorative epithet of 'Cockney'; not simply the foolish assumption of a capacity to write poetry in persons of inappropriately low birth and social standing, but a vulgarity in pretending to fashionable hankerings for the comfort and luxuries of nature from a too-obviously suburban perspective.

These elements are present here and elsewhere in Keats. But even this early in his development their presence makes for effects that are complicated by their context in the larger poetic conception, and that are certainly easy to distinguish from those of Hunt's own verse. For, while the stylistic influence is marked and in a sense unhelpfully derivative, Keats's larger formal conceptions in 'I stood tip-toe...' and 'Sleep and Poetry' are definitely odd and difficult to specify in terms of established models. The poems are essentially cast as verse letters, although without a specified recipient. Their tone is partly that of a kind of relaxed conversation, which is enthusiastic to share tastes and experiences, in literature, in a wider range of cultural interests, and in nature and other sources of physical pleasure. There is no narrative, except as the poem moves in loosely sequential fashion through a series of reflections on poetry, and on Keats's own relation to it. The overall effect suggests the excited sharing of hopes and aspirations as this might be done by young and newly intimate companions who have been drawn quickly together by the discovery of common enthusiasms, and the whole move forward in Keats's poetic growth that these poems embody clearly owes a lot to his recent immersion in new friendships and literary minds.

For all its Huntian mannerism, 'I stood tip-toe...' is the first authentically Keatsian poem. Its theme is the search for a theme, and its narrative is simply a kind of abstract development through areas of potential subject matter towards a style that might make its materials serve a grand design. Its form offers an image of Keats's effort to grow, through creative effort, into a poet, and the poem that emerges itself marks the stage of development at which Keats has arrived in producing it. The poem's ambition is declared in its attempt to serve as the induction of a long poem on the myth of Endymion (Keats for a while referred to the poem in progress as 'Endymion'), an attempt that peters out in speculative questioning that leaves the bigger task untried:

> Was there a Poet born? – but now no more,
> My wandering spirit must no further soar. –

> (ll. 241–2)

This pattern will be repeated; Keats works through his assimilation of an established poetic voice towards a distinctive new idiom, and this growing into his own identity is commensurate with a poem that ends as the effort to sustain thematic development founders. The poem's principal preoccupation thus becomes its own unfolding stylistic identity, and its narrative is the process of its own unfolding towards the limits of what Keats finds himself capable of achieving given his stage of development. It is poetry so insistently concerned with its own growth towards maturity that it serves perfectly, and with intriguing reflexivity, an emerging grand theme of the human experience of growth and change.

This theme in Keats from the start embraces his own development as a poet, but also his development as a thinking, feeling, and morally responsible person. And it will broaden to include larger questions of stability and change through historical time, and of the living writer's relation to literary traditions. These broader parameters are already clearly emergent in 'Sleep and Poetry'. In this poem a catalogue of 'luxuries' suited to poetic evocation, similar to the first part of 'I stood tip-toe...', leads into a celebration of 'poesy', but poesy as a realm in which Keats has not yet earned the right to live:

> O Poesy! For thee I hold my pen
> That am not yet a glorious denizen
> Of thy wide heaven –

> (ll. 47–9)

At first, this world of poesy to which Keats aspires appears to consist in the savouring of sensory and imaginative pleasures, chiefly consisting in beauties of nature filtered through, and mingling with, a rather naive picture-book version of the furniture of classical mythology. It is dangerously close to Leigh Hunt's aimlessly ornamental poeticizing. But Keats's intellectual reach and range seem to grow as the poem itself lengthens, and there is a distinctive turn to the projection of his own future career as a writer, which envisages his own development through this first youthful phase towards a sterner and much more ambitious engagement with the reality and scale of suffering human experience. And in so projecting this development, the poem itself begins to move that development forward, becoming the expressive form of a new maturity:

> O for ten years, that I may overwhelm
> Myself in poesy; so I may do the deed
> That my own soul has to itself decreed.
> Then will I pass the countries that I see
> In long perspective, and continually
> Taste their pure fountains. First the realm I'll pass
> Of Flora, and old Pan...

(ll. 96–102)

But the poem has already passed through this realm in its opening paragraphs, and moves beyond it in this résumé of its qualities. A further, darker territory is already coming into view, and as the poem seeks to characterize it so it starts to displace the first innocence of Keats's poetic identity:

> And can I ever bid these joys farewell?
> Yes, I must pass them for a nobler life,
> Where I may find the agonies, the strife
> Of human hearts –

(ll. 122–5)

The following lines use the symbolic figure of a 'charioteer' – adapted by Keats from a mythological landscape by Poussin – to embody his imaginative anticipation of the knowledge and experience, and the affective stylistic power, that will constitute his mature poetic identity. It is a strange vision (see lines 125–54), necessarily cloudy, and suggesting an adolescent's dream of adulthood, already shadowed by intimations of the reality of imagined experience. He cannot sustain it, and falls back into a new sense of his present person; but his reality is now troubled into changeful development, and the verse simultaneously moves into a new register, pulling more strongly against the beat of the rhyming couplets, and away from the stylistic attributes of the influence from Hunt:

> The visions all are fled – the car is fled
> Into the light of heaven, and in their stead
> A sense of real things comes doubly strong,
> And, like a muddy stream, would bear along
> My soul to nothingness: but I will strive
> Against all doubtings, and will keep alive
> The thoughts of that same chariot, and the strange
> Journey it went.

> (ll. 155–62)

The effort to imagine a more developed maturity, in terms both of poetic achievement and of personality, then leads into a further series of reflections on the English poetic tradition that Keats aspires to join, and, in joining, to become as it were its growing point. The literary history sketched in lines 162–229 is conventional for Keats's generation and immediate literary community, looking to Shakespeare and the early seventeenth century for inspiration and models, and deploring the supposed stiltedness and unhealthily French-influenced formalism of Pope and his followers:

> They swayed about upon a rocking horse,
> And thought it Pegasus.

> (ll. 186–7)

Keats's poem, as we have noted, is of course itself in rhyming couplets, and there is something callow in Keats's casual dismissal of the capabilities of a form that he is using as the very form of his attack. The comparison with Pope's own practice does not flatter Keats. But there are indications in the versification of both 'I stood tip-toe...' and 'Sleep and Poetry' that Keats's poetic ambition is grounded in the promise of real poetic originality. There is, for example in 'I stood tip-toe...', the striking note of a definite articulated confidence, catching the exact quality of a closely observed phenomenon, in the cadence of 'How silent comes the water round that bend' (recalling

Shakespeare's 'How sweet the moonlight sleeps upon this bank' in *The Merchant of Venice*), which breaks against the affectations of the preceding lines like a new voice:

> Linger awhile upon some bending planks
> That lean against a streamlet's rushy banks,
> And watch intently Nature's gentle doings:
> They will be found softer than ring-dove's cooings.
> How silent comes the water round that bend...

(ll. 61–5)

II

Abbey was infuriated by Keats's decision to give up medicine. According to his brother George's later account, Keats had by his twenty-first birthday in October 1816 sold two-thirds of his inheritance in trust with Abbey to meet the costs of his medical training, and was probably left with a legacy of little more than £500, giving an income of about £55 per year. Over the next eighteen months Keats must have spent more than his income from interest on the trust fund, and he also made a series of ill-advisedly generous loans, for example, to Haydon. Relations with Abbey worsened progressively over this period. In mid-November Keats and his brothers had moved to new lodgings at 76 Cheapside. Amongst Keats's many new literary friends was the bookseller and publisher Charles Ollier, introduced by Clarke, who was already publishing Shelley and declared himself anxious to publish this new rising young star. Keats began to think of making up a volume of his poems. He also continued to develop ideas for an ambitious long poem on Endymion, which had been touched on in 'I stood tip-toe...'. Through Christmas of 1816, and into the new year, further important contacts were established and strengthened. Keats dined regularly with Hunt, Horace Smith, Haydon, and Reynolds. In February Hunt showed his work to the Shelleys, William Godwin, Basil Montagu, and William Hazlitt. Keats was soon afterwards visiting and dining with the Shelleys. Keats and Hazlitt may already have become acquainted by now, probably meeting first through Haydon. Hazlitt was an established figure in literary London, and a regular contributor to the *Examiner*.

His conversation, lectures, and published criticism were to prove a powerful influence. In early 1817 Keats's thinking about art deepened in dialogue with Hazlitt and Haydon concerning the achievement of Greek sculpture in the Elgin Marbles, and the relation of reality to aesthetic ideals. He continued to write poetry, still concentrating on the sonnet, the preferred form of his poetic apprenticeship. In February two sonnets appeared in the *Examiner*, where he now began to publish regularly. Many others were produced in the autumn and winter of 1816 and the first months of 1817, mostly occasional in character, written to and about friends, often extemporized or produced feverishly overnight after an evening of excited talk. According to Clarke, one evening in late February, when the last batch of proofs of his first volume of poetry was brought for correction, Keats rapidly extemporized a dedicatory sonnet to Hunt, at 'a side-table, and in the buzz of a mixed conversation'.[2] *Poems* was published on 3 March 1817 by Charles and James Ollier, the first of the three books that Keats published in his lifetime. It contained nearly all the poems Keats is known to have written up to that date. 'I stood tip-toe...' follows the dedicatory sonnet to Hunt, and 'Sleep and Poetry' is the last poem in the volume. Sonnets, including the one on Chapman's Homer, but also others of widely varying quality, make up the rest of the volume, together with the Margate Epistles, and a number of other efforts in variously derived styles, but especially in a Spenserian manner (the 'Imitation of Spenser', and also 'Specimen of an Induction to a Poem' and 'Calidore'). Reynolds reviewed the *Poems* favourably in the *Champion* for 9 March, but no one outside Keats's immediate circle showed any interest. As Clarke bluntly remarked, the book 'might have emerged in Timbuctoo'.[3] Little more than a month later a disappointed Charles Ollier wrote indignantly to George Keats of his regret at having published the volume, which one dissatisfied purchaser had characterized as 'no better than a take-in'.[4] Ollier's irritation was no doubt heightened by Keats's surprising decision, almost immediately after the appearance of his first book, to change publishers. He probably met John Taylor around March 1817 through Reynolds, whose *The Naiads* had been published in 1816 by the well-established firm run by Taylor and his partner James Hessey in Fleet Street. Taylor was particularly interested in Keats's projected long poem on Endymion. It was doubtless through Taylor that Keats also first met Richard Woodhouse, a lawyer who acted as an informal adviser to Taylor & Hessey in matters legal and literary. Woodhouse quickly came to the settled view that Keats was a poet of genius who would one day be ranked with the greatest English writers. He set about accordingly to record for posterity, during the period of his friendship with Keats, and after his death, as much material as he could find relating to Keats's poetry. This material mostly survives and has become a principal source for our knowledge of Keats.

Probably at about this time, in March 1817, as Woodhouse recalled, one day when 'Keats and Leigh Hunt were taking their wine together...the whim seized them...to crown themselves with laurel after the fashion of the elder bards'. This light-hearted affectation was then discovered by visiting young ladies, on whose arrival Keats 'vowed that he would not take off his crown for any human being: and...wore it...as long as the visit lasted'.[5] The episode, which produced a series of weak sonnets, hints at what Keats would come to regard as a mannered, trivializing, and frankly embarrassing quality in Hunt's influence.

III

Once Keats had definitely given up his medical career, there was nothing to keep him near Guy's Hospital south of the river. Towards the end of March he moved north with his brothers to lodgings on the first floor of a house at 1 Well Walk in Hampstead, near to Hunt and his friends. The house belonged to Benjamin Bentley, the local postman. Keats was soon introduced by Reynolds to one of his Hampstead neighbours, Charles Wentworth Dilke. Dilke, six years older than Keats, was a tidy-minded civil servant in the Navy Pay Office, with educated literary tastes that included a great enthusiasm for Shakespeare. He had published an edition of *Old English Plays*, and from the beginnings of this friendship Keats himself began to read Shakespeare and his contemporaries with a new concentration. Keats also seems to have met James Rice and Benjamin Bailey around this time, again through Reynolds. Bailey had matriculated at Oxford in 1816 and was reading for holy orders. Rice was a young man in poor health, but the wit and fortitude with which he bore his illness earned Keats's admiration. The intimacy with Hunt and his friends continued, but other literary contacts were beginning to influence Keats. Shelley, just three years Keats's senior, had already published a good deal. His reputation was not high, but the *Alastor* volume had appeared a year earlier, with a title poem of a quality and ambition that placed Keats's own poetic achievements in a fresh light.

Keats now determined to test his abilities. He wrote to George that *Endymion* would be 'a trial of my Powers of Imagination and … invention … I must make 4000 Lines of one bare circumstance and fill them with Poetry'(L. i. 169–70). The task was probably conceived in direct rivalry with Shelley, whose *Laon and Cythna* was written over an almost identical period of time in the middle six months of 1817. Keats decided to leave London to attempt his project in solitude, and left for the Isle of Wight, perhaps at Dilke's suggestion, on 14 April, spending the night at Southampton before crossing to Newport. He visited Shanklin, then took lodgings at Carisbrooke. The fine sonnet 'On the Sea' was probably written on 17 April, but this was Keats's last sonnet for many months. Work on *Endymion* began immediately. He found difficulty in making a convincing start on the formidable project he had set for himself, and left the Isle of Wight to visit Tom in Margate towards the end of April. The 'Hymn to Pan' (*Endymion* I. 232–306) was written at this time, amidst worries about money that led to a loan of £20 from Taylor and Hessey.

In mid-May he sought a change of scene in Canterbury, remarking in a letter to his publishers that 'the remembrance of Chaucer will set me forward like a Billiard-Ball' (*L.* i. 146). This strikes the authentic tone of Keats's correspondence. Few letters survive from Keats's first twenty years, but thereafter, and particularly from the spring of 1817, there is abundant record of Keats's brilliance as a letter-writer. These letters articulate a personality of extraordinary critical intelligence, generous sympathies, and richly engaging tactful good humour, and are justly regarded as an achievement ranking almost with the poetry itself. Haydon noted Keats's 'exquisite taste for humour',[6] a quality that shines through his correspondence.

At the end of May Keats visited the village of Bo Peep near Hastings, where he met Isabella Jones. Keats's relations with women were never entirely comfortable. Woodhouse remarked that he had the 'idea that the diminutiveness of his size makes him contemptible, and that no woman can like a man of a small stature',[7] but he seems also to have found it difficult to take women seriously in intellectual terms, and to square the ordinary friendliness of social relations with his sexual drive. He admitted to Bailey that 'I have not a right feeling towards women' (*L*. i. 341). The extent of his actual experience of sex is a matter for conjecture, although there seems to have been some kind of sexual liaison with Isabella Jones at this time, and the opening of Book II of *Endymion* perhaps shows its influence. Some short lyrics from this period, such as 'Unfelt, unheard, unseen', also suggest recent sexual experience.

Keats returned to Well Walk on 10 June, and promptly borrowed a further £30 from Taylor & Hessey. Work on *Endymion* continued throughout the summer months. He read extracts to Clark and Severn in August. A draft of the first two books was complete by the end of the month. In the late summer Keats met Charles Brown, a former schoolfellow of Dilke's. Brown had a comfortable competence inherited from his brother, and had already composed a libretto for the comic opera *Narensky*, which had run for ten nights at Drury Lane in 1814. With Dilke he had built a double house in John Street, Hampstead, called Went-worth Place (later Lawn Bank, now Keats House). This was a significant new friendship, and over the next two years Brown became perhaps Keats's most intimate confidant and supporter. On 3 September, whilst his brothers were visiting Paris, Keats travelled to Oxford to stay with Bailey at Magdalen Hall, where he read Milton and Wordsworth, regularly took a boat on the Isis, and composed *Endymion*, Book III, at a steady fifty lines a day. The third book was finished before the end of the month, and after visiting Stratford-upon-Avon with Bailey on 2 October Keats returned to Well Walk and began work on the fourth and final book of his poem. He also resumed his metropolitan social life, with frequent calls on Hunt, Haydon, Reynolds, Brown, Rice, and the Shelleys, amongst others. In the second half of October he was confined at Hampstead with an infection developed at Oxford. He treated himself with mercury, conceivably for syphilis, but probably for gonorrhoea. More seriously, his brother Tom was very unwell by the end of the month. And Keats's public reputation took an ominous turn with the publication in October of the first of the *Blackwood's* articles on the 'Cockney School', in which 'Z' launched a virulent attack on Hunt. Keats was not mentioned in the article, but his name appeared in capitals in the epigraph. A review by George Felton Mathew of the 1817 *Poems* had appeared in the *European Magazine* in May, followed in June by a series of much more positive notices by Hunt in the *Examiner*. Verse by Keats had also been appearing regularly over the summer, in the *Champion*, the *Monthly Repository*, and the *Examiner*. The association with Hunt, who had famously been imprisoned for a libel on the Prince Regent, now began to draw genuinely hostile fire from the Tory reviewers. In the aggressive literary politics of the day, the 'Cockney' epithet denoted a metropolitan upstart and vulgar pretension. It was, as we have noted, aimed especially at Hunt, whose mannered style sorted awkwardly with a professed enthusiasm for Wordsworth. Keats was an obvious target as a well-known admirer and friend of Hunt, but the jibe also connected unfortunately with his supposed low social origins.

By the end of October Keats was planning to finish *Endymion* within three weeks, and after making further good progress he travelled on 22 November to Burford Bridge in Surrey, where at the Fox and Hounds Inn he finished the poem on 28 November after a final burst of sustained writing at eighty lines a day. The completion of *Endymion* is pivotal in Keats's poetic development. It can hardly be termed a success, and yet without it Keats's subsequent career could not have unfolded as it did. It is a project that bears all too obviously the marks of being forced, willed into being under the constraints of a schematic timetable, which Keats adhered to only by a consciously self-disciplining regime of invention and writing. As a result the mannered quality of his indebtedness to Hunt often becomes intrusively evident, and indeed almost parodic in taking the style to an extreme – as, for example, in the dominance of run-on lines – that far outdoes Hunt himself. The writing also often shows signs of a slack hurriedness (forced rhymes, abbreviated action, distracting epithets, conscious phrase making), particularly noticeable towards the end of each book, combined with an absence of narrative drive and clarity that makes sustained attentive reading very difficult.

And yet, *Endymion* does not quite fail, either. Keats's self-imposed trial of his own powers has to address directly the question of subject matter; there is a real sense in which all of his poetry up to the beginning of 1817 has taken as its main concern Keats's own fittedness for, and development as, a poet. As we have seen, this reflexivity is not unproductive, but it constantly, and self-consciously, begs the question of the true purpose and validity of a poetic vocation. There has to be a turn outwards to embrace the concerns of community, of social and political order, of tradition, and ultimately of an ethical dimension. But Keats was, and felt himself to be, still young, and his experience, personal, social, and educational, still relatively limited. Classical myth offered a means to explore wider territory, with its inherent burden of allegorical and symbolic suggestiveness and its universal currency.

In myth, Endymion, a young shepherd of Caria, is fallen in love with by Diana, Goddess of Chastity, after she sees him sleeping naked on a mountain top. Her modesty, symbolized in the moon with its enchanting but cool light, prevents her from any direct waking approach to Endymion, but she casts him in sleep and visits to kiss in nightly dreams. The myth in Keats's handling becomes a vehicle to express and explore the relations between earthly and ideal experience, and with its multiple ramifications and recurring motifs – the connection between imaginative experience and dreamful sleep, temporal and permanent modes of existence, pleasure and suffering – *Endymion* points forward to, and frequently anticipates, the preoccupations and distinctive handling of Keats's major work in 1818 and 1819. The poem's four books narrate the onset of a melancholy in Endymion, following his revelation in a dream vision of an ideal woman, which leads him to seek through the world for a means to union with her. This quest takes him under the earth (Book II), under the sea (Book III), and finally into the air (Book IV), and ultimately to a meeting with a real Indian maid for whom Endymion renounces his heavenly love, only to find her metamorphose into the goddess of his original quest. The poem may thus be interpreted to argue that the means to union with the ideal is through engagement with real earthly experience and suffering. This fits with the fact of the poem's clear intellectual indebtedness to Shelley's *Alastor*. In that poem

Shelley narrates the story of an intensely idealistic young poet whose career ends in failure, obscurity, and death, because his quest for union with an ideal visionary woman leads him away from all engagement with the realities of his actual earthly experience. The commitment to a transcendent ideal vision is thus represented as deeply destructive, if permitted to subordinate the claims and responsibilities of social and sensory experience. Shelley's unnamed visionary, like Keats's Endymion, meets and is fallen in love with by a real woman, an 'Arab maiden' (*Alastor*, 129–39), but Shelley's protagonist spurns her attentions in favour of the ultimately fatal pursuit of an unattainable ideal woman. In *Endymion* the hero's explicitly opposite choice, which is rewarded by the revelation that the earthly and ideal women are one and the same, appears as a direct responsive rehandling of Shelley's narrative.

But *Endymion* is too long. It cannot be read consistently as allegory, because its materials are too profuse, and the narrative too wanderingly protracted. Its deliberate seeking for a more engaged and responsible address to concerns beyond Keats's own does, however, push the poem towards a scale and seriousness that has the promise of what is to come over the next two years. Much critical attention has been paid to the poem's urging of a 'fellowship with essence' (i. 779), an ability to inhabit the reality of experience other than one's own, which leads, through increasing modes of intensity, to a oneness with the ideal. This notion is variously supplemented and elaborated throughout the poem, and in contemporary letters, to embrace the idea of what Keats famously described in a letter to John Taylor as the 'gradations of Happiness even like a kind of Pleasure Thermometer' (*L.* i. 218). Much has been made of this idea, which can perhaps be glossed as a quasi-Platonic conception of ascending levels of pleasure, which play off against one another in the complexity of the human drama. The image is characteristic of Keats's emerging critical-reflective manner in his correspondence, at once suggestive and thoughtful (and keenly observed, as here in the vivid application of a medical device), but also unsystematic, and lacking the consequitive coherence of formal thinking. It invites and stimulates thought, but as a formulation its confident air of authentic revelation is nevertheless oblique and creatively speculative. The effort of sustaining *Endymion* did, however, include this willed making of space for 'philosophizing', driving Keats to test and interrogate his intellectual reach, and by so doing to extend it.

The poem is animated also by other drives and tensions. Its eroticism is striking, and caused concern even amongst Keats's warmest supporters, such as Woodhouse. It explores the feelings released by Keats's own sexual experience, with Isabella Jones and presumably other women, and inaugurates a series of poems in which Keats's feminization of the ideal leads repeatedly to a blurring of sexual with other modes of desire. The blocked desire for an unattainable idealized woman becomes so often in Keats the form for other yearned-for unions that it can seem itself the displaced central preoccupation of his poetic and personal maturity.

For all its exasperating and at times almost unreadable stylistic affectation and mannerism, *Endymion* does now and then also look forward to, and occasionally actually articulate, a new level of achievement in poetic quality. The famous opening, 'A thing of beauty is a joy for ever', presents a courageous and undaunted defence of the necessity of art as a means to reconcile us to the pain and vicissitudes of

> despondence, of the inhuman dearth
> Of noble natures, of the gloomy days,
> Of all the unhealthy and o'er-darkened ways
> Made for our searching.

(I. 8–11)

The diction, phrasing, and movement of the whole passage are partly in thrall to Hunt: twelve of the first twenty-four lines are run on; four of the first six have weakly 'feminine' rhymes; some of the rhymes have an almost comically forced quality (a trait that laid Keats's earlier published verse particularly open to critical ridicule). But the tone is complex. The posed and artificial effects are mingled with that almost conversational manner established in 'Sleep and Poetry', the voice of an excitable and appreciatively savouring young intelligence, anxious and quick to learn, and to think about its knowledge. It is the voice of the letters, retaining their blend of rich good nature and thoughtful speculation with a rather hit-or-miss ambition to offer abstract and general formulations. It is from around this time that Keats's letters begin to extend their range to include a series of critical commentaries and sequences of thought that both inform, and often precede, his poetic developent, and that were taken up in twentieth-century Anglo-American literary criticism as amongst the most insightful and attractively sympathetic of all commentaries on poetry and the imagination by poets.

The opening passage of *Endymion* keeps its sense of the separate and differently existing realm of art in tension with the necessary dependence of art upon those very realities from which it is a form of escape. Keats's increasingly subtle and suggestive handling of this relationship, which holds together the apparently opposed realities of idealized imaginative experience, on the one hand, and, on the other, the hurtful mundanity of particular lives in real time, will quickly become the abiding concern of the major poems. Throughout *Endymion* the poetic voice only very intermittently achieves the distinctively Keatsian reflective writing of the opening, although the first half of the first book is relatively well sustained. Sometimes we can detect in the versification of *Endymion* the growing presence of Shakespeare, whom Keats was reading unceasingly through the composition of his poem, and whose inexhaustible variety of versification, and weight of phrase, often cut across the dominant style. Keats's wider reading in the Elizabethans – Drayton, Chapman, and Sandys's *Ovid*, for example – also becomes increasingly evident. The high point of Keats's poetic achievement in *Endymion* is undoubtedly the 'Hymn to Pan', which looks forward remarkably to the Odes of spring 1819. The 'Hymn' breaks out of *Endymion*'s rhyming couplets to take the form of a sequence of five stanzas, of successively fifteen, sixteen, sixteen, fourteen, and fourteen lines. The couplet rhymes are sustained, but slightly disturbed by commencing the first of these stanzas on the second rhyme of a couplet. The stanzas themselves are further varied by the shifting use of shorter lines of two or three feet, in the thirteenth and fifteenth lines of the first stanza, the last lines of the next two, the twelfth and fourteenth of the fourth, and the last line of the last stanza. All this variation strongly anticipates the experimentation with sonnet rhymes out of which the 'Ode to Psyche' develops some two years later, and which in turn immediately makes way for the more tightly organized variety of stanzaic pattern in the great Odes. The 'Hymn to Pan' celebrates the Greek mythic figure as an embodiment of the imagination itself, holding in still permanence the paradigm of all natural cycle and effect. Keats's evocation of this symbolic figure hints at the vocabulary and imagery that will haunt the Odes:

> O thou, for whose soul-soothing quiet, turtles
> Passion their voices cooingly 'mong myrtles,
> What time thou wanderest at eventide
> Through sunny meadows, that outskirt the side
> Of thine enmossèd realms: O thou, to whom
> Broad-leavèd fig trees even now foredoom
> Their ripened fruitage; yellow-girted bees
> Their golden honeycombs; our village leas
> Their fairest-blossomed beans and poppied corn;
> The chuckling linnet its five young unborn
> To sing for thee; low creeping strawberries
> Their summer coolness; pent up butterflies
> Their freckled wings; yea, the fresh budding year
> All its completions – be quickly near,
> By every wind that nods the mountain pine,
> O forester divine!

(I. 247–62)

The anticipation of the 'Ode to Autumn' is striking, not simply in the abundance of similar details and phrasings, but in the sharp attention to the fall of individual words and cadences within the pattern of the verse and the unfolding grammatical logic. There is too a kind of Shakespearian power of phraseology in combination with clear-sighted observation, as in the 'fairest-blossomed beans and poppied corn', the exactly 'five young unborn' linnets, the 'summer coolness' of the strawberries.

Once Keats had finished work on the first draft of *Endymion* in the inn at Burford Bridge, he wrote a letter to Bailey exploring 'the authenticity of the Imagination': 'The Imagination may be compared to Adam's dream – he awoke and found it truth' (*L. i.* 185). This arrestingly direct metaphor for the secular and earthly character of ideals in Keats's conception – that they are to be understood as deriving from the sources of earthly happiness, but 'repeated in a finer tone' – is a more telling and succinct articulation than anything in the 4,000 lines of *Endymion*. But the exercise of writing it had helped him to this clarity and ease of expression. There are some passages late in *Endymion* that are almost like versified examples of Keats's mature style as a letter-writer, such as, for instance, the passage in Book IV describing the 'Cave of Quietude' (IV. 512–62). This passage develops a complex metaphor for a state of mind that mixes the dark psychological condition of being conscious of the extent of suffering and pain, in one's own experience but also stretching far beyond it, with the passive and slightly chilled distance Keats associated with high creativity. Here *Endymion* also anticipates the writing and manner of the *Fall of Hyperion*. But once he had finished with the draining compositional timetable of his long six-months project, Keats very quickly realized that, having served to move him forward as a writer, it would not need to detain him. The process of copying out and correction was unusually rapid, and by the time he wrote its Preface, he was speaking of it as if long outgrown.

Keats returned from Burford Bridge to Hampstead around 5 December, and entered upon an increasingly busy social life, with new friendships and frequent visits to galleries, lectures, and the theatre. On 14 December he saw his brothers off on the coach to Teignmouth in Devon, where Tom was going for the sake of his health. Over the next few days Keats saw the actor Edmund Kean, whom he greatly admired and was said to resemble, in several roles, including Richard III. He began to produce a series of miscellaneous shorter poems, and fell into regular and friendly intercourse with James and Horace Smith, Lamb, Hazlitt, William Godwin, and Thomas Noon Talfourd. He attended the Royal Academy Exhibition on 20 December. The next day his review of Kean's acting appeared in the *Champion*. This heady mix of experience produced one of his greatest letters, when after a visit to the pantomime probably on 26 December with Brown and Dilke a discussion on the way home led to Keats's exposition in a letter to his brothers of 'Negative Capability', the quality that 'went to form a Man of Achievement especially in Literature and which Shakespeare possessed so enormously' (*L*. i. 193). Keats's famous letter characterizes this deftly coined phrase as 'when man is capable of being in uncertainties, Mysteries, doubts, without any irritable reaching after fact & reason'. This gloss exactly captures the growing intellectual confidence that followed the *Endymion* exercise, a confidence that, in conscious paradox, is able to countenance the limits of intelligence and reason in comparison with the power of art. Keats's 'Man of Achievement' in literature does not take sides, or seek to persuade, but offers insight into the feel of human experience by a chameleon-like ability to inhabit the reality of things other than self. Shakespeare's dramatic poetry is for Keats the supreme instance, but Keats himself was to find high critical esteem in the twentieth century for his own exemplification of this power. This view of Keats emerged in the work of the American New Critics, for whom the apolitical autonomy of poetry was in wider terms a major emphasis. Their criticism, and its successors, served to shape an image of Keats as pre-eminently the poet of pure form, offering a poetry perfect in its ironic, reflexive self-containment. But Keats was more than that. The 'Negative Capability' letter itself moves constantly between abstraction and quotidian detail, and between the chill permanence of art, and the transient intensity of the experience it draws on, and moves us to. He writes, for example, of a picture by Benjamin West that it represents 'nothing to be intense upon; no women one feels mad to kiss; no face swelling into reality. The excellence of every Art is its intensity, capable of making all disagreeables evaporate, from their being in close relationship with Beauty and Truth' (*L. i.* 192). The assertion of art's power as lying beyond 'disagreeables' is in fine tension with the restless drive of the prose to give the effect of that very 'intensity' we are supposed to leave behind. The subtle passion with which Keats now begins to explore this paradox drives his development with accelerating force.

It was probably at about this time, in late December 1817, that Keats was apparently stung by Wordsworth's response to his recitation of the 'Hymn to Pan' from *Endymion*, when according to Haydon 'Wordsworth drily said "a Very pretty piece of Paganism"'.[8] In Haydon's account Keats never forgave Wordsworth for this slight, if slight it was, although the circumstances and date of the incident are unclear. Another celebrated event involving both Keats and Wordsworth certainly took place on 28 December 1817, when Haydon gave his 'immortal dinner' for Keats, Wordsworth, Lamb, and Wordsworth's cousin Thomas

Monkhouse. After several hours of inspired talk the company moved to take tea, where they were joined by some invited friends. The evening reached a memorable comic climax in an exchange between Wordsworth and the Deputy Comptroller of the Stamp Office, who spoke to the great poet in such ludicrously inappropriate terms that Lamb was moved to a pitch of drollery at their expense that reduced Keats and the company to helpless laughter.

This busy social life continued into January and February. Keats attended 'a sort of a Club every Saturday evening' and was invited by Haydon to dine 'every Sunday at three' (L. i. 202, 204). He was a regular attender at Hazlitt's lectures. There were introductions to Henry Crabb Robinson, and, through the Shelleys, to Thomas Love Peacock, Thomas Jefferson Hogg, and Claire Clairmont. Freed from the discipline of his long poem, Keats now entered a freshly productive period. He had been seeing Wordsworth a good deal, and was reading the Elizabethans, under the influence of Hazlitt's lectures on the English poets. He now experimented confidently, and also returned to writing sonnets, in an assured and practised manner; 'On Seeing a Lock of Milton's Hair', 'On Sitting Down to Read *King Lear* Once Again', and 'When I have fears...' were all written at this time. On 4 February his sonnet 'To the Nile' was composed in a timed competition with Hunt and Shelley. Later in the month, on 27 February, he wrote to John Taylor of his 'Axioms' in poetry, that it should 'surprise by a fine excess', and that if poetry 'comes not as naturally as the Leaves to a tree it had better not come at all' (L. i. 238). Keats was correcting *Endymion* and preparing it for the press throughout this period. Book I was delivered to the publishers on 20 January, and Book II on 6 February. He finished the fair copy of Book III before the end of the month, and began on Book IV while reading proofs for the first three books. He had also begun *Isabella; or The Pot of Basil*, a narrative poem in *ottava rima* that was conceived in a project with Reynolds to produce verse tales from Boccaccio. Keats's own subject was probably suggested by Hazlitt. The poem represented a significant new departure, reaching for a sustained and studied complexity of texture he had not previously attempted.

But, as happened often in Keats's short life, this determined commitment to his maturing literary career was interrupted by personal problems. Tom had been spitting blood, but in spite of this George returned to London from Devon at the end of February, leaving Tom alone. George, whose behaviour now began to chime less perfectly with Keats's own best interests, had decided to marry and emigrate to America. Keats had little option at this short notice but to leave the preparation of *Endymion* to his publishers, asking Cowden Clarke to check proofs, and join Tom in Teignmouth. He left London by coach in a violent storm on 4 March, reaching Exeter on the 6th and arriving in Teignmouth the next day. He stayed at 20 The Strand (now Northumberland Place). The Keats brothers had been spending time in flirtatious friendship with the three daughters of a Mrs Jeffrey, 'the Girls over at the Bonnet shop' (*L.* i. 246) at 35 The Strand, and Keats fell in with this routine. It rained continuously for six days after his arrival. Keats was insulted at the theatre in Teignmouth on about 10 March, in obscure circumstances. Tom had a haemorrhage on the 13th. Money was short, and George sent £20 in the middle of March. In spite of these worries Keats managed to finish copying *Endymion*, Book IV, by the 14th, and on 19 March he wrote and dated a first preface to *Endymion*, sending it with the remaining copy to his publishers on 21 March. He learned on 9 April that his Preface had been rejected by Reynolds and his publishers, who feared that its apologetically defensive tone might expose him to public ridicule and attack. The next day he wrote and sent a new Preface. This was still defensive, but struck a valedictory note in bidding farewell to his own period of poetic apprenticeship. Keats's poetic career had reached a new level with the completion of *Isabella* around the end of April.

An advance copy of *Endymion* arrived in Teignmouth on 24 April. Within a month the poem was published in London by Taylor & Hessey, dedicated 'to the memory of Thomas Chatterton'. It met at first with little reaction beyond Keats's immediate circle, and even here responses were guarded. It seemed oddly constructed, and not always easy to follow in its adaptation of classical narrative. More worrying, for instance to Taylor, was the poem's sometimes fervid sensuality and its Hunt-like mannerisms of style. The volume sold poorly and was ultimately remaindered.

4

April–May 1818: *Isabella*

Isabella; or, The Pot of Basil has a tighter sense of narrative control, a more distinctive and independent stylistic identity, and a defter interweaving of symbol and story than anything Keats had hitherto written. It is also darker in feeling, and at once more confidently literary and more distinctly odd. The mannerisms that afflict *Endymion* and test the reader's patience are in *Isabella* evidently posed and conscious. The awkward rhymes, arch medievalism, and eccentricities of diction, phrasing, and syntax appear as parts of a deliberated stylistic texture; in comparison with all of Keats's preceding work, perhaps excepting the Chapman sonnet, *Isabella* has a much more focused and purposive tone. But it is nonetheless strange for that. Its grotesque plotting, taken from a tale in Boccaccio's *Decameron*, is turned by Keats to unexpectedly suggestive and complex thematic purposes. The tensions and paradoxes latent in his writing of the past year now animate a narrative manner that combines abstraction from Keats's own everyday social world, with a most telling, if oblique, commentary on the underlying contours of that reality.

The poem's dark side is foreshadowed in the verse letter that Keats wrote to John Hamilton Reynolds on 24 March 1818, from Teignmouth. This poem is in the relaxed conversational manner developed in the Margate epistles and 'Sleep and Poetry'. It begins as a light-hearted and fanciful effort to cheer Reynolds up on his sickbed. But after some sixty lines that recall 'Sleep and Poetry' in their evocation of escapist dream landscapes, prompted by imaginary scenes in literature and painting, the relaxed manner darkens and Keats acknowledges that his

51

delight in sensuous and imaginative pleasures cannot be easily sustained in face of the manifest contradictions, evils, and vexing mysteries of experience. This acknowledgement brings with it a change of stylistic key, as the established manner becomes more weightily reflective. The couplets are sustained, but the verse takes on the meditative movement of a Shakespearian soliloquy (recalling Hamlet in particular), which pulls against the light feel of the rhymes:

> O that our dreamings all, of sleep or wake,
> Would all their colours from the sunset take,
> From something of material sublime,
> Rather than shadow our own soul's daytime
> In the dark void of night.

(ll. 67–71)

This new sense of the inescapable promptings and questionings of mind is then arrested by a feeling of inadequacy – 'to philosophize/I dare not yet' – which is in its turn overcome by a kind of productive openness and perplexed honesty in the face of serious intellectual challenge:

> O, never will the prize,
> High reason, and the lore of good and ill,
> Be my award! Things cannot to the will
> Be settled, but they tease us out of thought.
> Or is it that imagination brought
> Beyond its proper bound, yet still confined,
> Lost in a sort of purgatory blind,
> Cannot refer to any standard law
> Of either earth or heaven? It is a flaw
> In happiness, to see beyond our bourne –
> It forces us in summer skies to mourn;
> It spoils the singing of the nightingale.

(ll. 74–85)

This sobered creative intelligence then turns back to a narrative manner, but now the story is of a moment of moral shock in the realization of the inescapable extent of suffering in the world. After such realization, Keats cannot go back to the conception of poetry as serving merely to pleasure and delight. It has to reckon with the relations obtaining between pain and pleasure, and, beyond that, to follow his hero Shakespeare beyond the negative capability of the chameleon poet, and into the tortuous ethical labyrinth of real experience:

> I saw
> Too far into the sea, where every maw
> The greater on the less feeds evermore. –
> But I saw too distinct into the core
> Of an eternal fierce destruction,
> And so from happiness I far was gone.
> Still am I sick of it; and though, today,
> I've gathered young spring-leaves, and flowers gay
> Of periwinkle and wild strawberry,
> Still do I that most fierce destruction see –
> The shark at savage prey, the hawk at pounce,
> The gentle robin, like a pard or ounce,
> Ravening a worm.

(ll. 93–105)

In *Isabella*, this savage vision of 'an eternal fierce destruction' transforms Keats's understanding, and representation, of imaginative idealism.

The poem tells of the love between Isabella and Lorenzo, whose mutual and dreamily self-absorbed infatuation is set against the coldly calculating mentality of Isabella's wealthy brothers. Their scheme to marry their sister off to a rich neighbour is threatened by her love for Lorenzo, who is employed by the brothers, and they devise a plot to murder him. Once Lorenzo is dispatched, his body is hidden in a shallow grave in a nearby forest, and after a period in which Isabella laments her absent lover she is visited by his ghost, who tells what has happened and reveals where he is buried. Isabella visits the grave with her nurse, exhumes the body, removes its head, and returns home to plant it in a pot in which she grows a basil plant. Her increasingly obvious distraction alerts the brothers to her discovery, and they disappear to banishment, leaving Isabella to her grief and madness.

This narrative embodies a set of thematic oppositions that now become central in Keats's work. On the one hand stand a range of valued experiences and conceptions: love, and especially young love that embraces a physical dimension; a luxuriant richness of sensory experience; the imagination and its projected forms, of dreams, ideals, art; and poetry itself,

standing especially as the supreme instance of creative activity
in a mode that can persist immutably against the depradations
of time. Against these positives are ranged the pragmatic,
workaday imperatives of real experience, limited in space and
time, subject to the rigour of rule and line and scientific
explanation, and to all the disciplines and necessities that are
variously contrary to desire and its fulfilment. But these
oppositions have often been misunderstood by Keats's critics
as too straightforwardly schematic, and it is important not to
miss the subtle ironies that Keats allows to play across them. The
historian E. P. Thompson, for example, has cogently formulated
these Keatsian oppositions, but with an overstated sense of their
mutually excluding enmity:

> This conflict [in Keats's poetry] sometimes appears as one between
> the sensuous and the philosophic life ('O for a life of sensations rather
> than of Thoughts!'), sometimes as between science and imagination
> ('Do not all charms fly / At the mere touch of cold philosophy?'): more
> often it is deeply embedded in the very structure of the poems
> themselves, in the acute tension between the richness of the life of the
> senses and imagination and the poverty of everyday experience, and
> in Keats's struggle to reconcile the two. It is his intense awareness of
> this conflict (which was of central importance to English culture),
> which gives greatness to his achievement.[1]

The problem with these persuasive formulations is that if they
are accepted then Keats's achievement is made to conform to a
cultural model of the 'Romantic' – with Keats as himself the
defining instance – which considers it a rejection of all forms of
social engagement. There is also a danger that the famous
declaration in an early letter, quoted glancingly by Thompson –
'O for a life of Sensations rather than of Thoughts!' – is taken as
a representative and inclusive rejection by Keats of the claims
and powers of intellect. It is in fact no such thing; the
exclamation comes in the letter to Bailey written in November
1817 (and discussed in the preceding chapter), just as Keats was
completing *Endymion*. It follows a passage in which Keats tries to
puzzle out the focused concentration required in the effort to
know the truth by 'consequitive reasoning', and, as one critic
has put it, the cry 'O for a life of Sensations rather than of
Thoughts' is that of a mind 'intensely burdened with thoughts'.[2]
The approach to Keats typified by Thompson implies Keats's

repudiation both of social engagement, and of argument itself, and suggests that, for all the idealism, the capacity for pleasure, and the intense power of human sympathy that prompt the wish to escape 'the poverty of everyday experience', Keats's poetry cannot usefully be read as an imaginative mode of positive engagement with the realities of his social life. But with the completion of *Isabella* Keats's development encompasses a more complex and self-demanding vision than can be contained by any such narrow conception.

At first sight, however, a schematized view of the thematic oppositions at play in *Isabella* can appear perfectly justified. The presentation of Isabella's merchant-capitalist brothers, for example, sets against the youthful sexual passion of Isabella and Lorenzo a coolly and grimly calculating spirit of mercantile enterprise. The brothers embody the heartless world of work and gain. It is through their agency that the sentimental idyll of the lovers is destroyed. And this interpetation of the poem's thematic pattern can justify a reading of the later main episodes, the visit of Lorenzo's ghost, Isabella's excavation of the grave and bizarre cultivation of her dead lover's head, as successive forms of lament for the loss of innocence, pleasure, and physical and imaginative fulfilment, under the inexorable pressure of social and economic exigencies. The oppositions embodied in the relationship between the brothers and the lovers in the poem may be broadened to encompass Keats's growing preoccupation with the claims of imaginative idealism as against rational empiricism. The lovers in the poem embody an idealism, founded on an imaginary conception of the good life in a close union of spiritual and physical modes of fulfilment, which is opposite to, and thwarted by, the cold, hard-headed pragmatic realism and financial acumen of the brothers.

But these oppositions do not work in any comfortably consistent way. Compare, for instance, the different ranges of knowledge and understanding displayed by the groups on either side of the opposition. There is an inward, excluding mutuality in the lovers' reciprocal absorption:

> Parting they seem'd to tread upon the air,
>   Twin roses by the zephyr blown apart
> Only to meet again more close, and share
>   The inward fragrance of each other's heart.

55

She, to her chamber gone, a ditty fair
  Sang, of delicious love and honey'd dart;
He with light steps went up a western hill,
And bade the sun farewell, and joyed his fill.

All close they met again, before the dusk
  Had taken from the stars its pleasant veil,
All close they met, all eves, before the dusk
  Had taken from the stars its pleasant veil,
Close in a bower of hyacinth and musk,
  Unknown of any, free from whispering tale.
Ah! Better had it been for ever so,
Than idle ears should pleasure in their woe.

(ll. 73–88)

The close intimacy of the lovers is sustained even while they are apart by a kind of entranced oblivion to other human society. Their mutually sustained apartness is insisted upon by the mannered repetition of the second quoted stanza, but it is also more subtly and more tellingly caught in the cameo representations of her solitary singing and his happily self-sufficient solitary walking. The verse makes us feel that even the poem's readers constitute the kind of unwelcome intrusion of a larger human society for which their love never wished to find a place. This almost wilfully self-blinding marginality to the wider range of human activity is in obvious contrast with the outlook of the brothers, who manifest a much more pervasive, observing cold scrutiny:

How was it these same ledger-men could spy
  Fair Isabella in her downy nest?
How could they find out in Lorenzo's eye
  A straying from his toil? Hot Egypt's pest
Into their vision covetous and sly!
  How could these money-bags see east and west? –
Yet so they did – and every dealer fair
Must see behind, as doth the hunted hare.

(ll. 137–44)

Clearly, the capitalist mentality of the brothers is offered as unattractive and limited. But it is not any more limited than the inwardness of the lovers. Indeed, the far greater range and manipulative capacity of the brothers' perspective is one way in which a certain *vulnerable* quality is suggested in the mode of experience that is nevertheless represented as the preferred mode of the poem's moral outlook. This vulnerability in the way that the lovers behave implicitly questions the viability of their idealism, and renders them almost culpable in their own fate. They invite the pragmatic manipulation that destroys them. The thematic opposition embodied in these contrasted outlooks is thus significantly modified. The power of an imaginative as against a rational mode of understanding is implicitly questioned by the poem's refusal to endorse without irony the experience of the lovers in the early stanzas.

It is a mark of the speed and quality of Keats's poetic development through the writing of *Isabella* that these thematic countercurrents have a corresponding level of stylistic contrasts. Parts of the poem are emphatically coloured by Keats's indebtedness to Hunt, and by his own deliberate refusal of a Pope-like polish and finish in the versification. The medievalism is elaborated with conscious relish, and the Italianate settings are imbued with a dreamy stage-Gothic by the obvious Englishness of the countryside. The poem is written in *ottava rima* stanzas (eight iambic pentameter lines, rhyming *abababcc*), but, in sharp contrast with other English practioners known to Keats, such as Byron or Fairfax, Keats's *ottava rima* avoids a sophisticated manner, and reaches instead for a quirky, idiosyncratic use of outlandish epithets, often in prominent rhyme positions. But now the apparent clumsiness, the uncultured and home-made quality of the writing, is emerging in a provocative controlled stylistic register, as Keats turns his struggle to build an authentic style into a truly distinctive new poetic voice. One notable feature of this voice is of a literal sense in the verse, which is constantly pulled about by the exigencies of awkward or eccentric rhyme-words:

'To-day we purpose, ay, this hour we mount
    To spur three leagues towards the Apennine;
Come down, we pray thee, ere the hot sun count
    His dewy rosary on the eglantine.'
Lorenzo, courteously as he was wont,
    Bowed a fair greeting to these serpents' whine;
And went in haste, to get in readiness,
With belt, and spur, and bracing huntsman's dress.

(ll. 185–92)

The striking and rather laboured rhymes here on 'Apennine' and 'eglantine' clearly work to import an Italian and medieval atmosphere, but they also establish a demand in the rhyme scheme, which is met in the phrase 'these serpents' whine', which seems at once grammatically forced and unluckily inapt (serpents don't whine). But the apparent crudeness of this is meditated and purposeful, and works in the context of Keats's increasingly confident rejection of a tradition of smooth facility in English versification. *Isabella* wears its awkward artifice on its sleeve, and suits its rhetoric to the pre-industrial freshness of its setting and materials. In its way it is as bold and challenging an intervention in English poetic language as the different, but related innovations effected by Wordsworth and Coleridge a generation earlier.

A newly characteristic Keatsian outlandishness of style is, however, balanced in *Isabella* by a quite different and contrasting manner, which appears carefully derived from the manner of Romantic mock-Spenserianism. This manner was a legacy of the satiric mock-Spenserianism of James Thomson's influential *Castle of Indolence* (1748), and had been used by Wordsworth in his 'Stanzas Written in my Pocket-Copy of Thomson's "Castle of Indolence"', with its famous portrait of Coleridge. The elements of this style included a combination of mock-archaic diction with details from the 'stock diction' of eighteenth-century nature poetry, and a deliberated narrative pace marked in the pattern of the Spenserian rhyme scheme. Byron had more recently used it in the opening stanzas of the first Canto of *Childe Harold's Pilgrimage* (1812), as the vehicle of a cynical and worldly-wise tone, slickly alert to the realities of human ways, and unillusioned about them. In *Isabella* the commercial world of the brothers is introduced by a striking variation of style that falls into exactly this idiom; the preceding stanza needs to be quoted, to demonstrate the abrupt and unmistakably calculated effect of Keats's shift in register:

> But, for the general award of love,
>   The little sweet doth kill much bitterness;
> Though Dido silent is in under-grove,
>   And Isabella's was a great distress,
> Though young Lorenzo in warm Indian clove
>   Was not embalmed, this truth is not the less –

> Even bees, the little almsmen of spring-bowers,
> Know there is richest juice in poison-flowers.
>
> With her two brothers this fair lady dwelt,
>   Enrichèd from ancestral merchandize,
> And for them many a weary hand did swelt
>   In torchèd mines and noisy factories,
> And many once proud-quiver'd loins did melt
>   In blood from stinging whip – with hollow eyes
> Many all day in dazzling river stood,
> To take the rich-ored driftings of the flood.
>
> (ll. 97–112)

The Spenserian manner is introduced emphatically in the prominently rhymed archaism 'swelt', and there is too a new industrial and productive reference in the diction – 'factories' – and an eighteenth-century habit of abbreviated grammatical forms suggesting a tendency to abstraction and personification ('from stinging whip', 'in dazzling river'). The style recurs with reference to the brothers, suggesting an entirely different mode of experiencing the world, which is much more far-seeing, workaday, and businesslike than the perspective of the lovers.

As with the poem's thematic oppositions, however, these contrasting styles are not patterned in any straightforwardly schematic way. The satirical, socially alert Byronic manner is indeed associated with the brothers, and steadily contrasted with the medievalism and natural-descriptive language used to characterize the lovers. But in the reading experience these contrasts are not clear-cut or mutually excluding. The poetry is working to register a direct sensory engagement with the real, in ways that are manifest on both sides of the supposed opposition. The brothers' exploitative merchant-capitalist mentality is given at times with a sensuous relish that properly belongs on the other side of the contrastive scheme, in, for example, the graphic detailed rendering of colour, and of physical movement and sensation.

Isabella represents an extraordinary jump forward in Keat's development, which to this day remains underestimated in the critical tradition. The subtle understated irony of his treatment of the lovers, in particular, demonstrates the rich rewards Keats was now reaping from the long months of labour over *Endymion*. Consider the lines that evoke Isabella's pining for the lost Lorenzo:

soon into her heart a throng
Of higher occupants, a richer zest
Came tragic – passion not to be subdued,
And sorrow for her love in travels rude.

In the mid days of autumn, on their eves
    The breath of Winter comes from far away,
And the sick west continually bereaves
    Of some gold tinge, and plays a roundelay
Of death among the bushes and the leaves,
    To make all bare before he dares to stray
From his north cavern. So sweet Isabel
By gradual decay from beauty fell,

Because Lorenzo came not.

(ll. 245–57)

This beautiful elegiac passage brings in a suggestion of the lovers' thwarted participation in the natural cycle. Imagery of warmth, seasonal fluctuation, and flowers, here as throughout the poem, does not serve straightforwardly to guarantee the rightness and naturalness of their relationship, but rather to dramatize its tragic dislocation from the recurring natural cycles that are the background to their experience. The effect of this is to ironize Keats's presentation of the lovers, thus delicately introducing a distance between them and the attentive reader. *Isabella* as a poem is conscious of dimensions in the experience of the characters, of which they themselves display no awareness. The brothers, certainly, cannot share in the lovers' order of experience. But they can discern it. The lovers, however, labour under an equally or even more limiting perspective, in that their experience blinds them to its antithetical forms. Their mutually absorbed assurance in love is assailable *per se*, in its willed and culpably vulnerable exclusion of the real. Its self-conscious, conventionally posed quality averts a true gaze not only on the activities and intentions of the brothers, but also on the true nature of their *own* experience, the physicality of sexual love. In discovering this kind of ironizing distance in Keats's treatment of the lovers we can also then better understand the purpose of the poem's opening stanzas, which give an elaborate account of the courtship of Isabella and Lorenzo. The manner of these lines is in fact firm but gentle parody, a delicate mocking of the young lovers' willing self-subjection to sentimental conventions of courtship. Their wan and pining attitude is in ironic contrast with the onset of high summer, as the days drift through 'A long month of May' up to 'the break of June', and their coy, embarrassed self-denials in the face of their own feelings are deftly marked in the imagery of illness – theirs is a 'malady', a 'sick longing' – and in the odd negative 'honeyless days and days did they let pass', which invokes the condition it denies.

In short, Keats's poetry initiates with the achievement of *Isabella* a searching critique of Romantic Idealism. The apparently innocent self-delusion and surrender to desire is revealed as self-destructive. In the harshly pragmatic, unloving, and profit-seeking real world of the brothers, an absorption in the conventions of sentiment makes for easy prey. The oppositions of *Isabella* establish a subtle perspective on the strange action; the dream world, aching for a realization of the perfect and the ideal, is destroyed by an uncongenial reality, but this destruction is in fact represented as a working-out of limitations inherent in the character of the dream world. The visit of Lorenzo's ghost is particularly interesting in this context. In sadly eloquent speech, the ghost evokes the marginalized social being of his speech:

> 'I am a shadow now, alas! alas!
>   Upon the skirts of human-nature dwelling
> Alone. I chant alone the holy mass,
>   While little sounds of life are round me knelling,
> And glossy bees at noon do fieldward pass,
>   And many a chapel bell the hour is telling,
> Paining me through: those sounds grow strange to me,
> And thou art distant in humanity.

(ll. 305–12)

The sense is of a radical dislocation from the purposeful business of the working world. Chapel bells tell off the hours ('Paining me through' beautifully gives the swinging rhythm and metallic resonant thrill of the chimes), as bees pass 'fieldward' and the air is filled with 'little sounds of life'. But Lorenzo is at the margins of this activity, a passive and remote observer, like one who lies bed-bound in illness as the day passes outside the window. He dwells on 'the skirts of human nature' (i.e. the outskirts), and his increasing distance from humanity is insisted upon in the repetition of 'alone'. This isolation is not a negation of his living experience, but a logical

61

extension of it; it dramatizes the inward-looking and unsocial character of his relationship with Isabella.

But other features of the description of Lorenzo's ghost point in another direction. The ghost's incipient physical decay is rendered with a disconcerting directness. This ghost is also a body who has been lying buried in the ground:

> It was a vision. – In the drowsy gloom,
>   The dull of midnight, at her couch's foot
> Lorenzo stood, and wept: the forest tomb
>   Had marred his glossy hair which once could shoot
> Lustre into the sun, and put cold doom
>   Upon his lips, and taken the soft lute
> From his lorn voice, and past his loamèd ears
> Had made a miry channel for his tears.

(ll. 273–80)

This is a more physically present Lorenzo than Isabella had been used to receive 'at her couch's foot'. The reality of his body is now eerily inescapable, with its 'glossy hair', 'loam'd ears', and face streaked through the mud with channels cut by tears. The full force of Keats's opening account of the conventionally sentimental courtship can now emerge. For it involved a denial of the body, of the physical and sensual basis of their attraction. Now that the real physical body is dead, the reality of love's sensory basis is cruelly brought home to Isabella. A strong erotic charge enters the poem in Isabella's half-deranged and obsessive efforts to recover the corpse (ll. 361–84), as, for example, in 'Her silk had played in purple phantasies', where the embroidered glove that Isabella recognizes is endowed with the suggestive power of a sexual dream. With this passage there is a decisive shift in the atmosphere of the poem. The reality of love and death is not now simply inescapable; Isabella's belated recognition of her sexual feeling for Lorenzo grotesquely exaggerates her own former illusions. Her 'infancy' has been 'school'd' (l. 334). She has learned to understand something of herself, and her world, but much too late. And, coming so much too late, her understanding serves horribly to mock her, in a manner reminiscent of the ironies of *Romeo and Juliet*, a play that haunts the language and conception of the whole poem.

II

On 1 May 1818, with *Endymion* and *Isabella* completed, Keats, still staying with Tom in Teignmouth, wrote an 'Ode to May' in fourteen irregular lines, hinting at achievements which lay a year ahead. Then over the next two days he wrote one of his most important letters, to Reynolds, in which Keats's mature manner as a letter-writer is fully emerged. It is by turns engagingly comical in warm sympathetic friendship; coloured by dark anxieties and forebodings, especially touching Tom's health; unostentatiously alert, informed, and serious in literary speculation, wide-ranging but particularly in consideration of the relative merits of Wordsworth and Milton; and, above all, it displays that distinctive Keatsian brilliance in developing self-analysis and speculative intellect, to articulate an accessibly untechnical engagement with existential problems. There is a definite new confidence in seeking to place intellect and the claims of knowledge: 'Every department of knowledge we see excellent and calculated towards a great whole ... An extensive knowledge is needful to thinking people – it takes away the heat and fever; and helps, by widening speculation, to ease the Burden of the Mystery: a thing I begin to understand a little ...' (*L*. i. 277). The 'Burden of the Mystery', of course, quotes from Wordsworth's 'Tintern Abbey', and anticipates the letter's famous central passage. But the reference to the 'heat and fever', the complicating counterclaims of body and health, sounds a theme prompted immediately here by Tom's increasingly serious illness, but also more widely by Keats's own experience and training as a doctor. It is not just that we are not free simply to act as creatures of knowledge and mentality, but that the physical and temporary conditions of existence require that we hold in relationship the different modes of body and mind. As the letter goes on to remark, 'axioms in philosophy are not axioms until they are proved upon our pulses: we read fine – things but never feel them to the full until we have gone the same steps as the Author' (*L*. i. 279). Keats goes on to elaborate a metaphor that gives powerful expression to this deepened awareness of the connection between a gathering sense of human suffering and its relation to great art:

I will put down a simile of human life as far as I now perceive it; that is, to the point to which I say we both have arrived at – Well – I compare human life to a large Mansion of Many Apartments, two of which I can only describe, the doors of the rest being as yet shut upon me – The first we step into we call the infant or thoughtless Chamber, in which we remain as long as we do not think – We remain there a long while, and notwithstanding the doors of the second Chamber remain wide open, showing a bright appearance, we care not to hasten to it; but are at length imperceptibly impelled by the awakening of the thinking principle – within us – we no sooner get into the second Chamber, which I shall call the Chamber of maiden-Thought, than we become intoxicated with the light and the atmosphere, we see nothing but pleasant wonders, and think of delaying there for ever in delight: However among the effects this breathing is father of is that tremendous one of sharpening one's vision into the heart and nature of Man – of convincing ones nerves that the World is full of Misery and Heartbreak, Pain, Sickness and oppression – whereby This Chamber of Maiden Thought becomes gradually darken'd and at the same time on all sides of it many doors are set open – but all dark all leading to dark passages – we see not the balance of good and evil. We are in a Mist – We are now in that state – We feel the 'burden of the Mystery', To this point was Wordsworth come, as far as I can conceive when he wrote 'Tintern Abbey' and it seems to me that his Genius is explorative of those dark Passages.   (*L.* i. 280–1)

This sketches a model of the development towards personal and poetic maturity. And, as is so often the case with Keats, the articulation of the sense of growing and changing itself takes that growth forward. The most telling moment here is the adaptation of a gothic frisson to give the feeling of being borne in upon by new intimations of suffering and soul-troubling anxieties, the realization that adult consciousness 'becomes gradually darken'd' as 'on all sides of it many doors are set open – but all dark all leading to dark passages'. In thus expressing a stage of development that is recognized as imminent, Keats actually writes the new stage in to existence.

Keats's immediate experience at this time did indeed offer newly threatening 'dark passages'. Life in Teignmouth had its attractions, including female admirers, a trip to Dawlish fair, and apparently a visit from his friend Rice. But everything was overshadowed by Tom's failing health. In spite of continued blood-spitting, Tom was determined to return to London. The brothers set off on 4 or 5 May, apparently accompanied by Sarah Jeffrey, one of the Teignmouth girls, as far as Honiton. At Bridport Tom suffered a serious haemorrhage, and the remainder of the journey proved slow, difficult, and distressing. They were back in Hampstead at Well Walk by 11 May.

5

May 1818–April 1819: *The Eve of St Agnes, Hyperion*

Throughout May 1818 Keats was 'very much engaged with his friends' (*L.* i. 286) in London. The idea of a walking tour in Scotland with Charles Brown had been under discussion for some time, and this now began to take shape. It was to provide materials for the further attempt at a long classical poem, which had been hinted in the published Preface to *Endymion*. This was *Hyperion*, for which Keats had undertaken serious reading, at Bailey's prompting, in Milton, Wordsworth, and Henry Cary's recently published translation of Dante. But once again concentration on literary projects proved difficult for Keats to sustain in the face of pressing distractions. His brother George married Georgiana Wylie on 28 May. Keats signed the register as a witness, troubled and depressed by George's imminent departure, the continuing difficulty of contact with his sister Fanny (still living under Richard Abbey's disapproving guardianship), and Tom's serious illness. Keats was himself unwell in early June. His doctor instructed him not to go out for several days. There were financial worries. Keats needed cash to cover the expenses of his walking tour. George had debts to clear and costs to meet before his voyage to America. Tom had hoped to travel to Italy for his health, but was clearly too weak for the journey, so money had to be found to pay Mrs Bentley at Well Walk to look after him in Keats's absence. All this put pressure on Abbey's trust fund, and on the mutual understanding of the three brothers.

The financial arrangements surrounding George's departure for America were to become a matter of serious controversy after Keats's death. George himself stated later that when he left for America he left his brother with nearly £300. This was later hotly disputed by Brown, who took George to mean that he had given money to Keats, whereas George probably meant that Keats had at that time some £300 of his own left in trust with Abbey. George had cashed his trust on coming of age in February 1818, and by his own account left £500 of the £1,600 cashed to clear debts and leave some means to his brothers. Keats lived on this money during and beyond Tom's illness. Although George's conduct, and his subsequent accounts of it, leave room for doubt as to his motives, it seems likely that Keats ended up owing George money, and that George, who had money problems of his own, did what he felt he could to assist his brother.

A different distraction loomed in the form of the reviews of *Endymion*. Keats and his friends were apprehensive that the Tory *Blackwood's Edinburgh Magazine* might continue its assault on Hunt by turning attention to Keats's published work. There were positive responses to *Endymion* from friends, and a favourable notice probably by John Scott in the *Champion*. But for the Tories Hunt's influence marked Keats out as fair game, and a critical storm was now gathering.

Keats left London for Liverpool with George and Georgiana Keats and Charles Brown on 22 June. They arrived in Liverpool on the late afternoon of the 23rd, and Keats and Brown set off on their tour early the next morning, taking the coach to Lancaster and leaving George and Georgiana asleep in the inn. Keats's brother sailed with his new wife for America a few days later.

Keats and Brown began their tour in earnest with a walk from Lancaster through the south lakes. Keats was disappointed to find Wordsworth out when they reached Rydal on 27 June, and disillusioned too when he learned that Wordsworth was on electioneering business for the Tory Lord Lowther. He was also struck by the prominence of Wordsworth's house and its familiarity to tourists. He nevertheless left a note for the poet, propped up on what he took to be a portrait of Dorothy, and after proceeding along Rydal Water to Grasmere was comforted by the humbler aspect of Dove Cottage. The walkers continued northwards, climbing Skiddaw on 29 June, then going on to

Carlisle, and from there by coach through Gretna Green to Dumfries. Keats wrote his sonnet 'On Visiting the Tomb of Burns' on this part of the journey. From Dumfries they walked westwards, from 2 to 6 July, first to Glenluce and then on foot and by mail-coach through Stranraer to Portpatrick. From there they took a boat to Donaghadee in Ireland, and walked to Belfast and back. Keats's letters to Tom and others recording all of this journey are wonderfully animated and graphic, including an extraordinary account of a squalid old woman, encountered on the way back from Belfast, carried in a filthy sedan chair 'like an ape half starved...in its passage from Madagascar to the cape...looking out with a round-eyed skinny lidded, inanity – with a sort of horizontal idiotic movement of her head...What a thing would be a history of her Life and sensations' (*L.* i. 321–2). They returned to Portpatrick on 8 July, walked via Stranraer to Ballantrae, and on to Girvan by 10 July, Keats producing here his sonnet 'To Ailsa Rock', and also completing the lines beginning 'Ah, ken ye what I met the day'. In its confident ballad-like metre and 'Scotch' diction this poem very cleverly reproduces the manner of Burns, and demonstrates that Keats now had at his command a considerable technical facility in verse. The poem also anticipates 'La Belle Dame sans Merci', in the combination of a ballad style with an oblique and suggestively abbreviated narrative. On 11 July they walked to Ayr, Keats quickly producing a sonnet whilst being shown round Burns's cottage, then on to Glasgow by the 17th, and through Inverary and up into the Highlands by the 19th, Keats writing verse all the time. He had declared himself dissatisfied with the sonnet he had written in Burns's cottage, and sought to do more justice to the event in another poem written at this time, the 'Lines Written in the Highlands after a Visit to Burns's Country'. The poem, again written partly as an exercise in an unfamiliar style, is in 'fourteeners', rhymed in couplets. It reflects on the experience of visiting places associated with a great dead poet. After an opening that seems simply to be relishing a tourist's pleasure in the atmosphere and associations of Burns's highland landscape, the reflective tone touches disturbingly on the dangers of abstracting oneself from reality by an intensity of concentration on the artistic achievements of the past. This abstraction is connected with fears of insanity, in the sustained detachment from immediate realities and a shared social and natural world, and such detachment comes to stand for the realm of art, with its pull away from time and place, its promise of emancipation from the personal and the particular. But the turn away from reality to art is potentially destructive, and Keats's own wariness of this dangerous attraction is implicit in his description of the immediate present realities in the local landscape, which are registered wth a sharp alertness that subverts the impulse to ignore them:

Light heatherbells may tremble then, but they are far away;
Wood-lark may sing from sandy fern, the sun may hear his lay;
Runnels may kiss the grass on shelves and shallows clear,
But their low voices are not heard though come on travels drear;
Blood-red the sun may set behind black mountain peaks;
Blue tides may sluice and drench their time in caves and weedy creeks;
Eagles may seem to sleep wing-wide upon the air;
Ring-doves may fly convulsed across to some high-cedared lair;
But the forgotten eye is still fast-wedded to the ground –

(ll. 13–21)

Keats goes on to articulate his dread of being tempted away from these realities. The fear inspired in the ring-doves by the circling eagle reminds us of the vision of nature in the 'Epistle to Reynolds', but the allure of travelling away from the suffering implicit in this real world, 'beyond the bourn of care,/Beyond the sweet and bitter world' (ll. 29–30) is resisted by our necessary human connectedness with time, place, and society: 'for at the cable's length/Man feels the gentle anchor pull and gladdens in its strength' (ll. 39–40). This refusal to think of art as an alternative to, or an escape from, the pain of experience was a commitment that Keats was now to find increasingly tested.

Keats and Brown had walked to Oban by 21 July, and next day caught the ferry to the Isle of Mull, where they took on a punishing thirty-seven-mile walk right across the island rather than meet the expense of sailing round it. On 24 July they visited Iona and Staffa by boat, viewing seascapes and land-scapes that made an obvious impact on Keats's writing. They rested in Oban, but Keats had developed a heavy cold in the crossing of Mull, and by the time the weary travellers moved on to Fort William on 1 August, climbing Ben Nevis on the following day, Keats was exhausted and suffering from an ulcerated throat brought on by bad tonsillitis. In Inverness a doctor declared Keats feverish and advised an immediate return to London. He took a coach to Cromarty and sailed on the smack *George* on 8 August.

II

Keats was back in Well Walk on 18 August. His doctor insisted that he be confined to the house. The sore throat was still bad, he was suffering from toothache, and he was also dosing himself with mercury, probably fearing that his ulcerated throat might have a venereal origin. Tom was now gravely ill. Brown's half of Wentworth Place was being rented by a young widow named Frances Brawne and her three children. Keats probably met the family around this time, but he was doubtless too worried by Tom's health to take notice of the eldest girl, Fanny, who was just 18. He made a copy of *Isabella*, and saw such friends as he could. Tom's condition offered little hope, and Keats's spirits received a further heavy blow with the appearance on 1 September of J. G. Lockhart's devastatingly offensive attack on *Poems* and *Endymion* in the August issue of *Blackwood's Edinburgh Magazine*, which concluded 'so back to the shop, Mr John' and ruthlessly pursued the jeering 'Cockney' epithet and all its associations.[1] This was followed on 27 September by J. W. Croker's attack on *Endymion* in the delayed April issue of the *Quarterly Review*, and at the same time Keats's *Poems* was savaged anonymously in the delayed June issue of the *British Critic*, which notoriously indexed *Endymion* as 'a monstrously droll poem'.[2] These attacks were plainly political in motivation, and aimed chiefly at Hunt. But they succeeded in sustaining a vitriolic and cruelly personal savagery at Keats's expense that has become legendary in literary history. His supposed low social origins were derided. His medical training became a running joke. His poetic ambitions, and even his lack of height, were ridiculed.

Friends offered assistance. Taylor and Bailey had tried to head off Lockhart's attack. An anonymous defence appeared in the *Morning Chronicle*, and Reynolds published a supportive notice in the *West of England Journal*, which Hunt reprinted in the *Examiner*. Keats himself, unwell as he was, and beset by personal difficulties and the imminent tragedy of his brother's death, made courageous efforts to maintain his composure in the face of this public onslaught. To an extent he succeeded. He was shaken and upset, but it is clear that his literary ambition and self-belief survived the crisis. He wrote to the George Keatses in mid-October, with a calm certainty, 'I think I shall be among the English Poets after my death' (*L*. i. 394). He was soon planning a new volume of poems with Taylor & Hessey, to include *Hyperion* as its cornerstone.

In the last week of September Keats was again confined to the house with a sore throat. Tom was weakening daily. Keats nursed him intensively, but also managed some socializing as October wore on, and continued to write verse. Haslam in particular proved an invaluable friend at this time. By mid-October he was working on *Hyperion*. On 24 October he met Isabella Jones again, and visited her apartment. Money worries continued to dog him. In the midst of all this he continued to write letters with an immense zest for life and intellectual subtlety. In a famous letter to Woodhouse of 27 October Keats distinguished his own 'poetical character' in contrast with the 'egotistical sublime' of Wordsworth; Keats's character as a poet

> Is not itself – it has no self – it is every thing and nothing – It has no character – it enjoys light and shade; it lives in gusto, be it foul or fair, high or low, rich or poor, mean or elevated – It has as much delight in conceiving an Iago as an Imogen. What shocks the virtuous philosopher, delights the camelion Poet. It does no harm from its relish of the dark side of things any more than from its taste for the bright one; because they both end in speculation. A Poet is the most unpoetical of any thing in existence; because he has no Identity – he is continually in for – and filling some other Body – The Sun, the Moon, the Sea and Men and Women who are creatures of impulse are poetical and have about them an unchangeable attribute – the poet has none; no identity – he is certainly the most unpoetical of all God's Creatures. (*L*. i. 387)

These remarks develop the notion of 'Negative Capability' from the letter to his brothers of the previous December. There is an engaging confident fluency now in elaborating this conception of the poet's unjudgmental openness to the world. Keats affirms an excited acceptance of the mix in things of good and evil,

71

pleasant and painful, and a definite sense of secure vocation in the readiness to embrace the inclusive breadth of experience. This is an essentially *dramatic* understanding of his own character as a poet, possessed of a power consisting in the ability to go out of itself to inhabit the reality of other personalities and things. It is in contrast with the Words-worthian personality, which absorbs experience in the service of self-expression, and which views experience in the reflexive light of massive self-projection. The letter is also wittily poised in consciousness of its own position, as Keats entertains the possibility that the very statement of such a position might then be understood as the opinion of a dramatically assumed personality, and not his own. But there is an urgent seriousness underlying the letter's friendly speculative tone. We sense an increasing drive to establish a poetic voice capable of maintaining in creative tension the co-presence of contradictory commitments and impulses.

Tom died on 1 December, and was buried in St Stephen's, Coleman Street, a week later. Keats, shattered by the trials of the past six months, gratefully accepted Brown's generous invitation to live in Wentworth Place. Regular social life could now begin to resume. On 5 December he attended the Jack Randall–Ned Turner prize fight at Crawley Hunt in Sussex. The friendships with Brown and Haslam grew still more intense, and Keats began to move in a wider circle once more. He also managed to see more of his sister, Fanny. To most of his friends, Keats appeared to possess comfortable independent means. They did not know he was living on money left behind by George, and that he was constantly importuning Abbey for advances. Nevertheless in late December Keats was offering to lend Haydon money. As Christmas approached he could not shake off his sore throat.

Keats was also seeing more of Fanny Brawne. He dined with the family on Christmas Day, and the couple came to an 'understanding', disapproved of by her mother because of her youth and Keats's uncertain prospects. Many amongst Keats's friends also disapproved of the relationship. Fanny struck them as superficial, vain, and flirtatious; and, although Keats clearly found her attractive and fascinating, he himself recognized a wilful affectation in her social manner. His doubts about the sincerity of her attachment often shaded into jealousy, and as his health began to fail these uncertainties led to sometimes unbalancing extremes of emotion. But Fanny was without question the great passion of Keats's life. The authenticity of her own feelings for Keats was long obscured after his death by the absence of documentary evidence, and the prejudices of nineteenth-century biography, which associated her influence with Keats's illness and decline.

Immediately after Christmas Keats had to postpone a trip to Chichester because of his sore throat, and was again confined for several days. He was somewhat better in January, which found him writing, and visiting. In spite of further financial worries, Haydon got his loan. Keats had to get £20 from Abbey before he could pay for his visit to Chichester in mid-January. Once there, in the midst of card parties and a visit to the Snooks (Dilke's sister Laetitia and her husband John) at Bedhampton, Keats managed to write most of *The Eve of St Agnes*. This poem effects a further startling leap forward in his development. The style has moved completely beyond Hunt's influence, which now, with the fast-growing consciousness of his own powers, comes to seem something of an embarrassment. Indeed, as Keats's emotional experience darkened, and his talent continued its quick ripening into greatness, disenchantment with Hunt's personality and style became suddenly obvious. *The Eve of St Agnes* offers a dazzling subtlety of versification in its brilliantly coloured Spenserian stanzas. There is a sensual relish for experience in the conception, phrasing, and diction, which transforms the poem's rich medievalism into a marvellously suggestive vehicle for the exploration of Keats's emerging central themes. These comprise the perplexing interconnectedness of pleasure and pain, good and evil, and the paradox of a human imagination in touch with things permanent and immortal, but itself dependant on the agency of a transient body. In the work on *Hyperion*, as we shall see, this theme widens to include a concern with history. The relationship between dreams and waking consciousness, associated always for Keats with the relation between ideals and reality, now becomes a particular and distinctive recurring preoccupation. Implicit in all of these, and gathering them together in the paradoxes of poetry itself, is the question of the relationship between art and life.

The Eve of St Agnes, like all of Keats's work up to January 1819, is an intensely literary poem; but there is a sophistication and assurance about its deployment of literary materials, which now serve the purposes of a wholly distinctive poetic voice. The 'gothic' trappings and atmosphere suggest variously the popular contemporary gothic novels of Mrs Radcliffe and M. G. Lewis, the historical romances of Sir Walter Scott, and Coleridge's 'Christabel'. But the dominant influence is undoubtedly from Shakespeare's *Romeo and Juliet*. The poem's narrative has a generalized English medieval setting, and concerns two feuding families, one of which is holding a ball in a castle on a cold winter's night. It is the Eve of St Agnes's day, 20 January; and we learn – or rather, in Keats's published version of the poem, have to infer – that a beautiful young lady of the family, Madeline, is observing a ritual customarily performed on this day. It is founded on the superstition that, if a young virgin maintains throughout the day a steadfast downward gaze, looking neither forwards nor to either side, but simply down at the ground, refrains from food, and goes to sleep having resolutely persisted in this ritual, then, in the words of a stanza drafted by Keats to help explain the plot (but not finally included):

> Twas said her future lord would there appear
> Offering, as sacrifice – all in the dream –
> Delicious food, even to her lips brought near,
> Viands, and wine, and fruit, and sugar'd cream,
> To touch her palate with the fine extreme
> Of relish: then soft music heard, and then
> More pleasures follow'd in a dizzy stream
> Palpable almost; then to wake again
Warm in the virgin morn, no weeping Magdalen.[3]

While Madeline is absorbed in this ritual, a young man named Porphyro belonging to the rival family, in love with Madeline and desperate for a sight of her, arrives secretly at the castle. Having grasped the situation, and with the assistance of Madeline's nurse Angela, Porphyro executes a scheme to take advantage of the ritual. He hides in Madeline's bedroom, and once she has fallen asleep he presents himself to her as if in a dream vision of her future husband. The poem reaches its brilliant climax in this moment of Madeline's awakening, in which her idealized imaginative dream of a heightened reality –

for we realize that she has been dreaming of Porphyro – effectively 'comes true' as she wakes up to find the real Porphyro at her bedside. But the poem's subtlety lies in the ambivalent handling of this climactic event. Keats's phrasing leaves the reader unclear as to whether, in the sexual consummation that evidently follows upon Madeline's waking, the young woman is indeed fully and self-consciously awake. There is the possibility that she understands herself to be fulfilling her dreamed-of desire for Porphyro actually within the fantasy of a continuing dream:

> Her eyes were open, but she still beheld,
> Now wide awake, the vision of her sleep –
> There was a painful change, that nigh expelled
> The blisses of her dream so pure and deep.
> At which fair Madeline began to weep,
> And moan forth witless words with many a sigh,
> While still her gaze on Porphyro would keep;
> Who knelt, with joinèd hands and piteous eye,
> Fearing to move or speak, she looked so dreamingly.
>
> 'Ah, Porphyro!' said she, 'but even now
> Thy voice was at sweet tremble in mine ear,
> Made tuneable with every sweetest vow,
> And those sad eyes were spiritual and clear:
> How changed thou art! How pallid, chill, and drear!
> Give me that voice again, my Porphyro,
> Those looks immortal, those complainings dear!
> O leave me not in this eternal woe,
> For if thou diest, my Love, I know not where to go.'
>
> Beyond a mortal man impassioned far
> At these voluptuous accents, he arose,
> Ethereal, flushed, and like a throbbing star
> Seen mid the sapphire heaven's deep repose;
> Into her dream he melted, as the rose
> Blendeth its odour with the violet –
> Solution sweet. Meantime the frost-wind blows
> Like Love's alarum pattering the sharp sleet
> Against the window-panes; St Agnes' moon hath set.
>
> (ll. 298–324)

One reading of these lines finds an endorsement of imaginative dreaming in thus waking to confirm the ideal as a heightened

75

repetition of reality. As Keats had written in the letter of November 1817 to Benjamin Bailey, 'The Imagination may be compared to Adam's dream – he awoke and found it truth' (*L*. i. 185). But this possibility is countered by the troubling implications of Porphyro's presence in Madeline's chamber. Has he cynically manipulated his way into taking advantage of her? His plan depends on the assistance of Madeline's old nurse, Angela, and Porphyro plays upon her alarmed concern to keep his presence in the castle a secret. The reader also wonders whether the whole scheme has been conceived by Porphyro in advance; he appears to know what date it is (ll. 115–17), and, although he then displays amazement when Angela explains Madeline's ritual, Keats's lines describing his conception of his 'stratagem' could imply an already fully-formed plan:

> Sudden a thought came like a full-blown rose,
> Flushing his brow, and in his painèd heart
> Made purple riot; then doth he propose
> A stratagem, that makes the beldame start...

(ll. 136–9)

The erotic charge of these lines also anticipates the discomfort of the climactic passage where Porphyro first watches Madeline undress, and then takes advantage of her commitment to her dream.

But it is, after all, a dream of Porphyro. The poem offers a representation of the unworldly vulnerability of a commitment to wished-for ideals, accessible through dream and imaginative experience. Porphyro takes advantage of Madeline's heedless conformity to the conditions of her dream. But the end result of his scheming is to provide a consummation in actual fact of the idealized fulfilment of which Madeline had been dreaming. And, in a poignant irony, his real person strikes Madeline with fear not because she realizes she has been taken advantage of, but because his physical reality appears to her as a reduced and ailing version of his heightened dream self:

> 'Ah, Porphyro!' said she, 'but even now
> Thy voice was at sweet tremble in mine ear,
> Made tuneable with every sweetest vow,
> And those sad eyes were spiritual and clear:
> How changed thou art! How pallid, chill, and drear!

terms the 'Ode to Psyche' grows out of Keats's now long-practised skill in the sonnet, as he begins the poem in an adaptation of sonnet rhymes to produce a complicated irregular form. The poem's preoccupation with the creative nurturing, gardener-like, of new growing varieties, is thus delicately shadowed in the Ode's own manifest formal genesis in a grafting of new stock on to old. The first fourteen lines do form a Petrarchan sonnet, except that Keats substitutes a trimeter line at line 12 – anticipating the use of this metrical variant in the stanzaic patterns of his more formal Odes – and he alters the last word of line 10 from the original draft reading, 'fan', to the unrhymed 'roof'. The last word of line 15, 'grass', is also unrhymed. The overall effect of this opening is of a poem that reaches for fresh formal possibility as the sonnet that had initially contained it breaks down in its final lines. No consistent stanzaic pattern subsequently emerges in the Ode, as it moves through a series of local variations on rhyme patterns of four, six, eight, and twelve lines, all derived from aspects of different sonnet types, and with a concomitantly unresolved metrical shape. The formal experimentation underlines the poem's feeling of striving for a breakthrough into new formal identity, and subtly endorses Keats's interest in exploring his own relation to the authority of an inherited literary culture.

The 'Ode to Psyche' is a profoundly reflexive poem, concerned with the processes of its own making. Its rhetoric is subtle and elusive. The goddess Psyche was born a mortal, but deified by Jupiter as a result of her love for Cupid. He was the son of Venus, who had killed Psyche for taking him away. The 'lateness' of her elevation to the gods meant that she was never worshipped amongst the Greek pantheon, and Keats develops this circumstance in making her the embodiment of the secular imagination, and identical with poetry itself, as the creative activity in which mortal humans may yet, in a post-religious age, find immortality. The opening lines need thus to be understood as an address to the creative power that is both itself the source of the poem, and its addressee; the Ode is in this literal sense about itself, a celebration of the unfolding poem that takes as theme the special status and value of its own emergent shape:

> O Goddess! Hear these tuneless numbers, wrung
> By sweet enforcement and remembrance dear,

> And pardon that thy secrets should be sung
> Even into thine own soft-conched ear.
>
> (ll. 1–4).

This opening section then offers a vision of Psyche and Cupid, imaging the possibility of union between human and immortal in a setting that merges imaginative dreaming with the sensual detail of a real natural world existing in time and space – in short, a complex image of the poem's own conditions of existence. The Ode develops this reflexive rhetoric by the elaboration of a language of worship. The goddess Psyche is the presiding spirit of the poem, which shapes itself as an expression of quasi-religious homage to that spirit. The Ode becomes a temple to the poetic creativity it embodies, with the poet Keats as priest of the temple, and this conceit builds to an extraordinary closing stanza:

> Yes, I will be thy priest, and build a fane
> In some untrodden region of my mind,
> Where branchèd thoughts, new grown with pleasant pain,
> Instead of pines shall murmur in the wind:
> Far, far around shall those dark-clustered trees
> Fledge the wild-ridgèd mountains steep by steep;
> And there by zephyrs, streams, and birds, and bees,
> The moss-lain Dryads shall be lulled to sleep;
> And in the midst of this wide quietness
> A rosy sanctuary will I dress
> With the wreathed trellis of a working brain,
> With buds, and bells, and stars without a name,
> With all the gardener Fancy e'er could feign,
> Who breeding flowers, will never breed the same:
> And there shall be for thee all soft delight
> That shadowy thought can win,
> A bright torch, and a casement ope at night,
> To let the warm Love in!
>
> (ll. 50–67)

The fane that Keats builds is, of course, essentially a mental construction, and is envisioned as set within an interior landscape that widens and complicates the workings of the metaphor. The poem is a product of intelligent artifice, set amid a forested mountainous scenery that evokes the vastly wider realm of consciousness as a whole. The growing point of this consciousness is the poem, conceived as shaped into new existence by a deliberated pruning, 'branchèd thoughts, new grown with pleasant pain'. The idea of this interior mental landscape as the setting in which the poem itself has been cultivated gains a further dimension by the glancing allusions in Keats's formulation to contemporary medical images of the brain stem as it is revealed in dissection. But Keats's deployment of the landscape as an image for consciousness offers no easy reading. The 'dark-clustered trees' and 'wild-ridged mountains' suggest remote and inaccessible reaches of mind, lying far outside the self-bounded and controlled arena where the poem has taken shape. In this setting Keats dramatizes his achievement in creating the Ode as a winning of order and beauty out of a surrounding wildness. This complex metaphor of landscape-as-consciousness recalls other major Romantic efforts to use the relations within an observed landscape to stand for the relations between landscape and the perceiving consciousness, and is no less powerful in evoking the difficult paradoxes of the self-conscious mind than, for example, Wordsworth in 'Tintern Abbey', or Shelley in 'Mont Blanc'. The apparently effortless fluency with which the closing image is developed, with the poetic imagination glimpsed as 'the gardener Fancy', creating new varieties by graft and hybrid variation, ironically belies the tremendous effort that the 'Ode to Psyche' in fact cost Keats (see *L.* ii. 105–6). The poem's last lines, where the poem is figured as a window left open and lighted on a summer night, to attract the butterfly Pysche in, beautifully catch the strengthening sense that Keats has found his way to a poetic form that can articulate his great central themes: the interdependence of art and reality, the immutable and the temporal, and the perpetual co-presence of transcendent abstract archetypes with specific historical circumstance, and the fleeting individual life.

II

Over the next few days after completing the 'Ode to Psyche' in late April 1819, Keats further explored the possibilities of the sonnet, expressing his frustration with its limits in 'If by dull rhymes our English must be chained'. Then, at the beginning of

May, the themes of the 'Ode to Psyche', and the formal experimentation of the preceding weeks, were brought to a poised focus in the 'Ode to a Nightingale'. In Brown's later account, a nightingale had nested near Wentworth Place, and Keats

> felt a tranquil and continual joy in her song; and one morning he took his chair from the breakfast-table to the grass-plot under a plum-tree, where he sat for two or three hours. When he came into the house, I perceived he had some scraps of paper in his hand, and these he was quietly thrusting behind the books. On inquiry, I found those scraps...contained his poetical feeling on the song of our nightingale.[1]

But Brown's famous narrative of the writing of the 'Ode to a Nightingale' is profoundly misleading. It suggests an unpremeditated burst of writing, thrown off in passing and all but discarded on completion; but everything about Keats's poem suggests otherwise. It inaugurates the central group of three Odes, 'Nightingale', 'Grecian Urn', and 'Melancholy', all composed in quick succession in May 1819, and which all share defining features of versification, diction, and theme. They build on the achievement of the 'Ode to Psyche' by moving through a series of very carefully organized variations on the formal patterns created in the break through in that poem from sonnet rhyme sequences. This fully emerged Keatsian Ode takes on the formal stanzaic arrangement of something like a short, intense, and tightly organized series of abbreviated hybrid sonnets. The 'Nightingale' stanza, like that of both 'Grecian Urn' and 'Melancholy', is precisely regular in repeating its ten lines. Each of these three odes uses the quatrain of a Shakespearian sonnet for its first four lines, and Keats then works subtle variations on the six-line sestet of a Petrarchan sonnet. Thus the rhyme scheme in 'Nightingale' is *ababcdecde*, perfectly regular through its eight stanzas. It proves a poetic vehicle very exactly suited to Keats's purpose in establishing a verse idiom that combines the sense of purposeful forward movement, with a feel of statuesquely arrested poise. This in turn serves the larger intellectual question that underlies Keats's whole extraordinary achievement in writing the Odes; how are we to negotiate the paradoxes and ironies of the fleeting direct personal knowledge of experiences and ideas that exist in timescales immeasurably greater than that of the individual human life? We seem to apprehend as fixed and permanent the informing values of a life that is caught up, inescapably, in the flow and movement of time, just as the verse of the Odes is always, simultaneously, offered as a static and completed object for contemplation, and a temporally unfolding verse movement. This is a problem about the personal relation to the great and permanent archetypes of existence, but the problem is partly comprised in the uncertain nature of those archetypes. Are pleasure and pain, love and the other dominating emotions, beauty and truth, a set of absolutes of which we are allowed, at best, only a transient experience? Or are these apparent absolutes in fact dependent for their experiential reality on the actual experience of individual people? And might they perhaps not after all be absolutes at all, but historically and culturally relative? In one aspect, this is, centrally, also a problem about history, and the individual's relation to historical process. Understood in this way, the Odes, for all their ostensible yearning for escape from the ordinary conditions of human existence into the timeless and pain-free realm of art, are themselves concerned, fundamentally, with history.

The form taken in the Odes by this deep concern with history embodies a decision to refuse history as the dominant ground for meaning. It is important to insist on the manifestly meditated character of this decision in the Odes. If we attempt to 'historicize' Keats – which is to say, seek an explanation of his poetry by looking to place it in its contemporary historical context – then that will involve a search for direct or indirect historical reference of various kinds, in an effort to weave the poetry back into its original complex relations with the wider culture and society that informs and produced it in the first place. This effort, however, is effectively a kind of patronizing of Keats, which misses the sophisticated and deliberated judge-ments on this way of interpreting human experience that make up the formal substance of the poems. That formal substance is developed as an attempt, ironically self-limited and self-aware as it is, to escape the conditions of temporality, to exist out of time.

Keats's Odes as a group are strikingly programmatic. The diction is remarkably consistent, the formal experimentation with variations on sonnet-derived elements is, as we have seen, systematic and progressive, and the themes circle round and connect up with each other in what seems a definitely deliberated way. Even the titles participate in this effect of homogeneity: Psyche, Nightingale, Grecian Urn, Melancholy, Autumn. These titles name a variety of things that form a set in being known to individual people, and known through the successive generations of people, but that are things neither existing in the same way as people, nor themselves dependent for existence on any one particular agency of their being. Nightingales as a species, for example, demonstrate all the qualities of behaviour and song that Keats notes in his Ode; those qualities do not depend on any one actual nightingale. Psyche as a myth exists in her narrative as immortal, and those narratives do not depend on particular acts of narration for their continued existence and transmission through time. Autumn as a season exists quite apart from the vagaries of a particular autumn; and so on. The fact that such things as this do not exist in the same way as individual people, and yet form part of the existence of individuals, constitutes a recurring dimension in experience of connectedness with orders of being that are out of human time. Keats is himself very well aware that poems themselves exist like this, as indeed do literary works in general. One of the things about reading something read before by countless others, in different times and places, is that the relatively general reference of the text is silently endorsed by the widely disparate human conditions to which it has spoken. This is a complicated part of one's reading experience of major works that have lasted, and all of the Odes conduct an implicit commentary on their own mode of existence in broaching the issue. In 'Ode on a Grecian Urn' the theme is fully explicit, in a beautifully concise and almost definitive formulation.

W. B. Yeats picks up the commonality of the set in the titles of the Odes in his sequence 'Meditations in Time of Civil War', from his volume *The Tower*, that is concerned amongst other things with the continuing life enjoyed by poems, and poets, through the influence they exert on the poets and poems which succeed them in a tradition. Yeats's many allusions to Keats's Odes in the volume thus themselves embody this thematic dimension. Yeats's titles are, for the most part, just like Keats's in naming things that persist far beyond the lifespan of the humans for whom they are significant: Ancestral Houses, My House, My

Table, My Descendants, The Road at my Door, The Stare's Nest by my Window; but then finally 'I see Phantoms of Hatred and of the Heart's Fullness and of the Coming Emptiness'. This last title is, obviously, categorically different. It displaces the various kinds of non-human temporality embodied in the preceding titles with the distracting immediacy of a current political crisis, and the possible outcomes of it, with their power to vex the imagination.

The rhetoric of Keats's Odes may be understood as a carefully meditated grammatical disengagement from the pressures of such local urgencies; in particular, the poems manipulate verb tenses in such a way as constantly to remove the articulated experience from any real historical time. In some cases the very presence of a main verb is debatable, so strong is the resistance to a fixing of the events of the poem in some relation to time. The opening stanza of 'To Autumn' is odd in this respect, as is the opening of 'Ode on a Grecian Urn'. The 'Ode to a Nightingale' begins in a present that is immediately displaced by an imaginary subjunctive, which is thereafter the dominant verb form:

> My heart aches, and a drowsy numbness pains
> > My sense, as though of hemlock I had drunk,
> Or emptied some dull opiate to the drains
> > One minute past, and Lethe-wards had sunk.
> 'Tis not through envy of thy happy lot,
> > But being too happy in thine happiness –
> > > That thou, light-wingèd Dryad of the trees,
> > > > In some melodious plot
> Of beechen green, and shadows numberless,
> > Singest of summer in full-throated ease.

(ll. 1–10)

The verb forms in these famous lines all serve to denote an action or state as conceived, rather than as fact, and, to adapt from the *OED* definition of the subjunctive, they express wish, command, exhortation, or a contingent, hypothetical, or prospective event. The actual present experience that we understand to be that of the speaking subject of the poem is confined to the opening line and a bit. The whole of the Ode's second stanza continues in this subjunctive tense, imagining what is not actually happening:

Oh, for a draught of vintage! that hath been
Cooled a long age in the deep-delvèd earth,
Tasting of Flora and the country green,
Dance, and Provençal song, and sunburnt mirth!

(ll. 11–14)

'Vintage' is a suggestive word here. Like other striking words in the Odes it denotes the product of temporally local and materially fleeting ingredients that can with the right skills be gathered and given a new form that transforms them and makes them last. In these properties 'vintage' shadows the properties of the poem itself, which builds to a form that can stand to time just as the nightingale's song does as it is invoked in the poem.

But the formal character of Keats's Odes is nothing if not ironic. The straining to find an articulation of the permanent absolutes that inform our experience, with its pull away from the passage of time, is in constant counterpoint with the forward impetus of the metrical texture in the verse itself. The Odes are simultaneously perfectly still, and perpetually moving, in their very formal identity as poems. The 'Ode on a Grecian Urn' develops this formal duality with a clarity and assurance that makes it the almost definitive instance of the self-reflexive poem, interrogating the claims and limits of its own mode of being in the world. The apparent recommendation of the ideal perfection of art, embodied in the urn (but also, implicitly, in the Ode itself), is ironized by the suggestion that its abiding fixity denies the essential reality of human joy and fulfilment, which is defined in process and can exist only as a function of time and change. The poem explores this paradox with a compacted fluency, charged everywhere with subtle implication and demanding reaches of thought, that confirms Keats's emergence as a great poet. Unlike the Psyche and Nightingale Odes, the voice that speaks the Grecian Urn Ode is not in the first person, but in a carefully neutral and descriptive second person, at once addressing and evoking the attributes of the urn, including its human narratives. This grammatical device, which is also deployed in the 'Ode on Melancholy', secures the impersonality of Keats's perspective, in a marvellous expression of the point of intersection of fleeting human reality with a poetic articulation that both preserves and falsifies experience. It is impossible within the limits of the present discussion to do justice to the detail with which Keats works through this central paradox; but notice, for example, the haunting evocation of the 'little town' in the 'Ode on a Grecian Urn' which, in being caught and fixed by the imagery of the urn at a moment when it has no living inhabitants, delicately shadows the condition of art itself, which can defy time, but only by relinquishing that teeming purposive occupancy and flux that gives life its meaning:

> What little town by river or sea shore,
>   Or mountain-built with peaceful citadel,
>   Is emptied of this folk, this pious morn?
> And, little town, thy streets for evermore
>   Will silent be; and not a soul to tell
>   Why thou art desolate, can e'er return.

(ll. 35–40)

7

June 1819–February 1821:
Lamia, 'To Autumn',
The Fall of Hyperion

I

Towards the end of May 1819 Keats was again unwell and obliged to stay at home. Money worries returned yet again. In April he had remarked to George that he 'was not worth a sixpence' (*L.* ii. 93). By the end of the month he was thinking of moving to Teignmouth, or becoming a ship's surgeon.

On 8 June Rice called and invited Keats to accompany him to the Isle of Wight. By mid-June Keats was speaking of himself as engaged, and broke. He saw little of the Dilkes from now on, as they openly disapproved of the relationship with Fanny. On 16 June he learned that Mrs Midgley Jennings was filing a bill in Chancery against the Keats family, and asked Haydon and others for the return of loans. Haydon's refusal annoyed him. Keats and Rice left on the Portsmouth coach on 27 June in a violent storm. They crossed to the Isle of Wight and settled in Shanklin. He sent love letters to Fanny Brawne, and wrote verse constantly through late June and into the first week of July. Keats was in an irritable state of health, but had completed the first part of *Lamia* by mid-July. Brown joined them in Shanklin, and Keats worked with him on a drama, *Otho*. He also began to revise and rework *Hyperion* as *The Fall of Hyperion*. With Brown's arrival the party fell into a routine of late nights and cards, placing further strain on Keats's health. Rice left towards the end of August, and Keats was left alone for a while in Shanklin while Brown travelled about the island. Keats was now deeply immersed in several major poems simultaneously, and writing with the confident fluency of an artist at the height of his powers. On Brown's return, they decided to visit Winchester, primarily to gather materials for Keats's poetic projects. On 12 August, with *Lamia* half-finished, they left Shanklin, narrowly missing an accident in the crossing from Cowes.

The first four acts of *Otho* were completed by 14 August. Keats now broke off his friendship with Bailey, who after courting Reynolds's sister had married someone else. He wrote to him for the last time on the 14th, expressing his ambition to 'make as great a revolution in modern dramatic writing as Kean has done in acting' (*L.* ii. 139). In fact the psychological tensions and insights of *Lamia*, and the complex self-interrogation of *The Fall of Hyperion*, suggest an almost novelistic quality in Keats's still-emerging powers.

Lamia completes, with *Isabella* and *The Eve of St Agnes*, the series of three major longer narrative poems that complements the achievement of the Odes in Keats's *œuvre*. The poem begins with the story of the god Hermes and his love for a nymph of fabled beauty. The Nymph has been rendered invisible by Lamia, who was herself once a woman but has been imprisoned in the body of a snake. Lamia is in love with a youth of Corinth, but she cannot consummate her passion whilst in her snake form, so she proposes to Hermes that she will make the nymph of his dreams visible, in return for a woman's form. He agrees to this, and Lamia promptly makes the nymph appear. The nymph's apparition is described in terms that once again rehearse Keats's recurring preoccupation with the relation of dream to reality, which itself figures his deeper engagement with the competing claims and interconnectedness of art and experience. For the gods, immortality and knowledge of the ideal are possible:

> It was no dream; or say a dream it was,
> Real are the dreams of Gods, and smoothly pass
> Their pleasures in a long immortal dream.

> (ll. I. 126–8)

The main narrative of *Lamia* is thus framed by a story that illustrates the impossibility for mortals of lasting happiness or fulfilment, by contrasting the essentially human tale of Lycius and Lamia with a happy fable of the gods. Hermes and his nymph immediately enter together a realm of perfected and permanent happy relationship, which slips out of the real, recalling the disappearance into the storm of Madeline and Porphyro at the end of *The Eve of St Agnes*:

> the God fostering her chillèd hand,
> She felt the warmth, her eyelids opened bland,
> And, like new flowers at morning song of bees,
> Bloomed, and gave up her honey to the lees.
> Into the green-recessèd woods they flew;
> Nor grew they pale, as mortal lovers do.

(I. 140–5)

The main narrative of *Lamia* works on two levels, involving the same kinds of oppositional thematic terms that we have noted as present throughout Keats's poetry; and here as elsewhere these thematic oppositions are more complex and less cut and dried than they can be made to seem in critical formulation. On one level, the poem is an account of a recognizable human relationship, the progress of a love affair; and, on another level, it is at the same time a parable of the imaginary in its destructive conflict with scientific rationalism and the domination of our commonplace social experience.

As a love story *Lamia* is a remarkable departure for Keats. The reader comes increasingly to set aside Lamia's half-mythical nature in the poem's handling of her unfolding relationship with Lycius. Early on, we view the relationship through her eyes, and in the assumption that she is practising an evil deception on the young man by concealing her serpent identity and making him fall for her by a dark magic. But this perspective gradually shifts, until quite quickly her blended person, half-real, half-illusion, comes to embody her attractive female self as perceived by the besotted Lycius. In other words, her combination of reality and illusion is offered in psychological verisimilitude as typical of the object of any human passion. People fall in love with real people, on to whom they project a fantasy of desire. The poem in fact becomes increasingly sympathetic to Lamia. Whereas at first her manner with Lycius is hard to get, playing the goddess in mock-cruelty and feigned indifference (for she has, of course, engineered their

98

first encounter in order to initiate a relationship), once their relationship is established it is Lycius who first grows tired of their intense enclosed self-absorption, and hankers for a return to wider social intercourse and a 'normalization' of the relationship by publicly celebrated marriage. In keeping with the markedly Byronic tone of the opening lines of Part II, Lycius not only grows beyond the spell in which Lamia has bound him, but quickly adopts a rather unpleasantly self-confident independence that pushes him to something like a triumphing in her discomforted awareness that he has become dominant in the relationship:

> The lady's cheek
> Trembled; she nothing said, but, pale and meek,
> Arose and knelt before him, wept a rain
> Of sorrows at his words; at last with pain
> Beseeching him, the while his hand she wrung,
> To change his purpose. He thereat was stung,
> Perverse, with stronger fancy to reclaim
> Her wild and timid nature to his aim:
> Besides, for all his love, in self-despite,
> Against his better self, he took delight
> Luxurious in her sorrows, soft and new.
> His passion, cruel grown, took on a hue
> Fierce and sanguineous as 'twas possible
> In one whose brow had no dark veins to swell.

> (II. 64–77)

Lycius's tutor Apollonius has been suspicious from the start of Lamia's origin and true identity, and it is his appearance at the marriage festivities – which Lamia has all along resisted and dreaded – that precipitates the disastrous revelation of her dual nature. This leads to her own vanishing, and to Lycius' death. In terms of the poem's psychology, Apollonius is the rational, unconvinced side of Lycius himself in his relationship with Lamia, which ultimately prevails in a stripping-away of Lamia's magical appeal, thus destroying her power.

Apollonius is also, in the other plane on which the poem works, of course associated with rationality and a hard-headed sense of the real workaday world; and particularly he associates with scientific knowledge, understood as destructive of imagination and wonder. The poem famously attacks the 'philosophy' (that is to say, 'natural philosophy' or science) of the Newtonian analysis of the spectrum in this context:

> Do not all charms fly
> At the mere touch of cold philosophy?
> There was an awful rainbow once in heaven:
> We know her woof, her texture; she is given
> In the dull catalogue of common things.
> Philosophy will clip an Angel's wings,
> Conquer all mysteries by rule and line,
> Empty the haunted air, and gnomèd mine –
> Unweave a rainbow, as it erewhile made
> The tender-personed Lamia melt into a shade.
>
> (II. 229–38)

But it is important to recall that, notwithstanding the attractive endorsement implicit in Keats's epithet of 'tender-personed', Lamia is, after all, truly a serpent in woman's form, and her attempt to love in a human world does end in catastrophe, both for herself and for the young man she entangles. The poem is in short intriguingly ambivalent on both sides of its apparent principle thematic opposition, entering profound critical reservations as to the respective claims both of scientific rationalism, and the power of the imagination.

Keats's versification in Lamia brilliantly underpins the pervasive ambivalence of the poem's values. It is written in heroic couplets, but the sense of tightness and strong control that is characteristic in that form is in constant tension with a deliberate exoticism of diction, and an extravagantly adventurous handling of pause and rhythmic variety. Consider for example the description of Lamia as a snake:

> She was a gordian shape of dazzling hue,
> Vermilion-spotted, golden, green, and blue;
> Striped like a zebra, freckled like a pard,
> Eyed like a peacock, and all crimson barred;
> And full of silver moons, that, as she breathed,
> Dissolved, or brighter shone, or interwreathed
> Their lustres with the gloomier tapestries –
> So rainbow-sided, touched with miseries,
> She seemed, at once, some penanced lady elf,
> Some demon's mistress, or the demon's self.
>
> (I. 47–56)

The grammar is run across the couplets here sometimes in an antithetical manner reminiscent of Dryden, and the overall sense of controlled syntactic complexity gives an assured and deliberated effect. This ensures that the odd abundance of sensual epithet, the general strangeness of conception, do not sound mannered or affected, but strike the reader as subordinated to the distinctive tone, and manifestly in the service of a subtle and meditated narrative style.

The critique in *Lamia* of imagination is perhaps the most sustainedly subtle that Keats produced. Lamia herself embodies those contrastive extremes of human experience – pleasure and pain, immortality and human time, art and life – which Keats repeatedly represented as essentially inextricable and mutually defining, but which in her are unnaturally separated out and distinct:

> A virgin purest lipped, yet in the lore
> Of love deep learnèd to the red heart's core;
> Not one hour old, yet of sciential brain
> To unperplex bliss from its neighbour pain,
> Define their pettish limits, and estrange
> Their points of contact, and swift counterchange;
> Intrigue with the specious chaos, and dispart
> Its most ambiguous atoms with sure art...

(I. 189–96)

This reads as a deliberate contrast with the celebratory account of the inseparability of pleasure and pain, joy and sorrow, in the third stanza of the 'Ode on Melancholy'. The passage underlines Lamia's fatally compromising ambivalence, offering all the charmed power of the imagination in love, but also dangerous in its distortive and unsustainable fantasy.

II

Keats completed *Lamia* in late August and early September 1819 in Winchester. His drama *Otho* had been finished by 23 August; he was also continuing work on *The Fall of Hyperion*, and revising *The Eve of St Agnes*. He was now desperately short of money. He borrowed from Hessey, and from Haslam. Brown left for Chichester around 7 September. Keats was distracted from his writing by a letter from George and hurriedly returned to London by the night coach on 10 September. His visit was brief but busy, with trips to the theatre, and meetings with Woodhouse, Hessey, and Abbey. He managed to see his sister on the 13th, and on the same day witnessed 'Orator' Henry Hunt's triumphal entry into London. He returned to Winchester two days later. The ode 'To Autumn' was written in Winchester on about 19 September. This was his last major poem, and perhaps his best. In formal terms the poem picks up from the innovation of the Odes written in May, and introduces a small but exactly considered mutation of the ten-line stanza form. 'To Autumn' has an eleven-line stanza, managed in such a way as to introduce a teasingly complex variation; the effect is of a quickening sense of the numerous possibilities that are freed by even a slight movement away from the constraints of classical sonnet rhyme. The first stanza opens with a conventional Shakespearian quatrain, but the second group of four lines (that is, lines 5–8) has three rhymes, *cded*, with the *c*-rhyme repeated in a couplet in lines 9 and 10, and a final rhyme on *e*. This pattern is then varied in the second and third stanzas, which share a second quatrain rhyming *cdec*, with the couplet in lines nine and ten rhyming on *d*, and a final rhyme on *e*. Keats had tested out this kind of variation in the rhyme scheme of the five stanzas of the 'Ode on a Grecian Urn', which, unlike the perfect regularity of the 'Ode to a Nightingale', employs three different variations on the ten-line shape (the first and fifth stanzas match, as do the third and fourth, with the second stanza offering a unique variation). And then, after the regular three-stanza shape of the 'Ode on Melancholy', he had again tried a series of variations in the 'Ode on Indolence'. But with this final effort in 'To Autumn' Keats reconsidered the effects he had been working with, and achieved the perfect balance of formal shifts within a basically fixed shape.

This balance of movement and stillness lies at the heart of 'To Autumn'. Many critics in recent years have focused on the poem as raising in pure form the problem of Keats's relation to history. The Ode was written about a month after the notorious Peterloo Massacre in Manchester, an event around which controversy still raged. Keats's possible preoccupation with this event, and the momentous political charge it carried, has been discerned as the

complementary absent reference implied by the poem's atmosphere of tensed expectant brooding. It could also be argued
that a more direct connection is present in the description of
how a personifièd Autumn's 'hook' momentarily 'spares the
next swath'. This might suggest the militia laying about the
heads of the people at the meeting with their swords, from
horseback, as depicted, for example, in George Cruikshank's
famous contemporary cartoon. It has also been argued that the
poem has an immediate resonance in the bad harvests in
England in the years leading up to 1819.

These are certainly possible contexts for a more exactly
historical dimension in 'To Autumn' than might at first appear;
but to argue for their presence as a function of a historicizing
reading of the poem surely misses the point. 'To Autumn' is
without doubt concerned with questions of time and permanence. It is an essentially historical poem in its central theme of
the relation between the impermanently alive and the timelessly
abstract and inorganic. It is a kind of irrelevance to ask whether
or not there is any quasi-specific allusion in 'To Autumn' to
Peterloo, or any other such specific historical circumstance,
because the poem is actually about the fundamental issues
raised by the instants when long-term or effectively timeless
aspects of experience intersect momentously with fleeting actual
events. 'To Autumn' circles around the vexing question of the
mode of presence in events of considerations and values that
precede and outlast them. The poem's evocation of the season of
change from verdant maturity to winter is precisely focused to
embody the paradoxes of such intersections. Autumn is a
permanently recurring phenomenon, at once in constant
process from just-begun to almost-over, and yet permanently
existing in our conception of the seasonal round as a
determinate sequence. The paradoxical union of movement
and stillness, arrested just at the moment when ripeness tips
into decay, stands as the most perfected image in Keats of the
way in which individual experience flickers through the
paradigm of large historical movements and generic human
experiences. The poem's own mode of existence offers a tacit
demonstration of the balance it strikes between movement and
stillness. Our reading experience is of a sequence, a forward
movement of syntax with a metrical identity and rhythmic pulse

that are synchronic in character, but that in coming to conclusion does not exhaust the poem or in any meaningful way 'end', because the poem continues to exist, and moves through its unfolding form afresh with each new reading, whether by individual readers, or by successive generations of readers.

III

By 21 September Keats had given up his revision of *Hyperion* because of its excessive Miltonic inversions; 'English ought to be kept up' (L. ii. 117). *The Fall of Hyperion* survives as a difficult fragment. It differs from the earlier incarnation of *Hyperion* in suggesting a Christian rather than a classical frame of reference, posing with a more troubled persistence and moral curiosity the ethical questions underlying Keats's decision to give up his career in medicine, and commit himself to poetry. As Keats finally abandoned it, *The Fall of Hyperion* consists of one completed book, and a start of some sixty lines on a second book. It incorporates, or begins to, the same treatment of myth in *Hyperion*, but within the new framework of a vision in a trance or dream. This is an important and telling structural modification, which Keats uses to good effect in returning to the question of the purpose of poetry as posed in his handling of the figure of Apollo. The main substance of *The Fall of Hyperion* in fact consists in Keats's more sustained examination of this question: is the poet no more than a socially and morally irresponsible dreamer? The dream structure ironizes his examination by grounding the whole quest for insight within a poetic vision that implies the special power of that kind of vision. Keats's continuing self-questionings concerning his vocation nevertheless produce a somewhat unresolved and obscure allegory, in which the poem's unfinished nature seems to owe quite as much to nervous intellectual uncertainty as to a dissatisfaction with the grand Miltonic manner of the first version. The character of Mnemosyne in *Hyperion* is replaced in the *Fall* by the more mysterious figure of Moneta, a female goddess around whom Keats develops an involved dream allegory. He finds himself granted a special kind of life exclusive to those who feel deeply the human condition, more enduring than, and exempt from, the vicissitudes of ordinary mortality. But Moneta nevertheless questions the poet-dreamer's value to humanity, implying that the visionary perspective is ultimately self-centred and undirected towards real social benefit. The poet-figure in Keats's vision then replies, self-deprecatingly, that, although he is not himself worthy, the truly great poets are surely the supreme physicians:

> Sure not all
> Those melodies sung into the world's ear
> Are useless: sure a poet is a sage,
> A humanist, physician to all men.
> That I am none I feel, as vultures feel
> They are no birds when eagles are abroad.
>
> (I. 187–92)

Here a general anxiety about the importance of poetic vocation blends with Keats's own more acutely personal uncertainty and self-doubt. But once again, for the last time in his poetic career, the effort to articulate a theme sufficient to justify Keats's commitment to his talent itself becomes the sought-for theme. *The Fall of Hyperion* is powerfully expressive of this very tension between the aesthetic and the moral in art, and in the life of the artist. The poem does not build towards the execution of a grand vision, but it does not quite falter either, but breaks off having developed towards a strange vision of Moneta. This vision encompasses in enigmatic and elusive terms the realization that the great poet must move through pleasure to human responsibility and an engagement with human suffering. At the same time, it stands as the incarnation of the artist's special mode of insight, 'an immortal sickness which kills not', taking us beyond suffering to the chilly dispassionate permanence of art:

> Then saw I a wan face,
> Not pined by human sorrows, but bright-blanched
> By an immortal sickness which kills not;
> It works a constant change, which happy death
> Can put no end to; deathwards progressing
> To no death was that visage; it had passed
> The lily and the snow; and beyond these
> I must not think now, though I saw that face –
> But for her eyes I should have fled away.

105

They held me back, with a benignant light,
Soft-mitigated by divinest lids
Half-closed, and visionless entire they seemed
Of all external things – they saw me not,
But in blank splendour beamed like the mild moon,
Who comforts those she sees not, who knows not
What eyes are upward cast.

(I. 256–71)

IV

By the end of September, with his revision of *Hyperion* finally abandoned, and his money worries deepening, Keats thought of giving up poetry. He was considering a career in journalism. Brown rejoined him in Winchester at the beginning of October from Chichester, where he had illegally married his housekeeper. Keats and Brown returned together to London after a week. Keats saw Fanny Brawne on 10 October for the first time since June. He took lodgings at 25 College Street, Westminster, in order to live cheaply, but also to avoid living next door to Fanny. An obsession with her was beginning to take hold, and the College Street plan collapsed. After only a few days he again visited the Brawnes, spent two days with the Dilkes, left his lodgings, and returned to Wentworth Place with Brown by around 21 October. Severn called on him a few days later and found him 'well neither in mind nor in body'.[1] It was possibly at this time that he wrote the sonnet 'Bright star! would I were steadfast as thou art', probably inspired by Fanny Brawne. This was long considered his last poem, because he wrote it out in Severn's copy of Shakespeare on the voyage to Italy in September 1820.

November 1819 found Keats struggling to borrow money. Haslam once again provided assistance. He got money from Abbey for the first time in ten months. On 5 November Keats missed a lecture in which he was quoted by Hazlitt. He visited friends in London, and dined out regularly. On the 17th he announced in a letter to Taylor his determination 'not to publish any thing I have now ready written'; he hoped to try for a few poems 'at home amongst Men and women', which would 'nerve me up to the writing of a few fine Plays' (*L*. ii. 234). He was reading Holinshed's *Chronicles*, and working on a new play, *King Stephen*, perhaps with Kean in mind. This work continued into December, when he also began a Byronic poem entitled 'The Cap and Bells', and apparently attempted one last revision of *Hyperion*. Just before Christmas he learned that *Otho* had been accepted by Drury Lane for the following season. On 22 December he wrote that he had been, and continued, 'rather unwell' (*L.* ii. 238). On Christmas Day, the anniversary of his first 'understanding' with Fanny, their engagement was formalized. His attempt to 'wean' himself from her in the autumn had failed. From this time Keats's passion for Fanny ran increasingly out of control as his health and hopes fell into terminal collapse.

Keats's brother George arrived from America on 9 January 1820. He believed himself to have been swindled by the American naturalist John James Audubon, and with a young family found himself in serious financial straits. Keats dined with him on his arrival, and embarked on a round of social and business visits that brought the brothers into contact with many old friends. George drew his remaining legacy from Abbey, together with most of the money remaining to Keats in the Abbey Fund, as this too was owing to him as a result of the financial arrangements made before his departure for America in June 1818. This left Keats in an extremely difficult financial position. George set off once more for Liverpool on 28 January, after seeing his brother for the last time. On 3 February, a bitterly cold day, Keats returned home to Hampstead late from town, travelling outside on the stagecoach to save money. He was feverish, and Brown realized immediately that he was seriously ill. As Keats retired to bed he coughed slightly, and Brown heard him say ' "That is blood from my mouth." ... he was examining a single drop of blood upon the sheet. "Bring me the candle, Brown; and let me see this blood." After regarding it steadfastly, he ... said, – "I know the colour of that blood; – it is arterial blood; – I cannot be deceived in that colour; – that drop of blood is my death-warrant; – I must die." '[2] He suffered a massive haemorrhage later that night.

Keats was confined for the rest of the month. In the middle of February he offered in anguish to break his engagement to Fanny. Barry Cornwall kindly sent books. He tried to proceed with 'The Cap and Bells'. Fanny sent a ring at the end of

February, and assured him that she still wished to marry him. By early March he was suffering violent heart palpitations, but his doctor was optimistic about his condition by the 8th, and he was declared out of danger on the 10th. He started to work again, revising *Lamia* for his planned new collection. He dined with Taylor on the 14th. But a week later he had suffered several further attacks of heart palpitation. He did manage to get out in late March and early April, and attended a private view of Haydon's 'Christ's Entry into Jerusalem' on 25 March. In April he was even planning a visit to Scotland with Brown. Taylor & Hessey received the manuscript of Keats's new volume of poems on 27 April. By the beginning of May he had given up the idea of accompanying Brown to Scotland. Brown had let Wentworth Place for the summer, so Keats took lodgings at 2 Wesleyan Place, Kentish Town, near to Hunt. Brown settled some debts for Keats and lent him money. Keats moved into his new lodgings on 6 May, and then travelled with Brown on the smack to Gravesend, where they parted for the last time.

In the first half of June Keats was correcting proofs, and still making social visits. He had a serious attack of blood-spitting on 22 June, and was obliged to move into Hunt's house in Mortimer Terrace. He continued to spit blood for several days. It was now obvious to everyone, and above all to Keats himself, with his medical training, that he was gravely ill, with the same 'consumption', or tuberculosis, that had killed his mother, uncle, and brother. During this period, in the last week of June, Taylor & Hessey published Keats's *Lamia, Isabella, The Eve of St Agnes, and Other Poems*, including all of the major odes, and *Hyperion*. Keats defiantly identified himself on the title page as 'the author of Endymion'. This collection is now recognized as amongst the most important works of English poetry ever published. Over the following weeks the book was widely noticed, generally in favourable terms. Jeffrey reviewed it enthusiastically together with *Endymion* in the *Edinburgh*, and began to redress the shameful injustices of Keats's earlier critical reception.

Keats's time was now short. Shelley's friend Maria Gisborne saw him at Hunt's in early July 'under sentence of death'.[3] His doctors had ordered him to Italy. After mid-July, he was too ill to write. His jealous passion for Fanny Brawne became a torture of frustrated desire and thwarted hopes. He fell out angrily with Hunt over some supposed slight, and moved out on 12 August to live with the Brawnes in Wentworth Place for the month leading up to his departure for Italy. On this same day he received a generous invitation from Shelley to stay with him in Italy. Keats courteously declined. It was not clear who would accompany him to Italy, or where he would live, and he waited in vain for news on this matter from Brown. Abbey refused Keats money towards the end of August. By 30 August, after another haemorrhage, he lay in a dangerous state. On 11 September he dictated to Fanny Brawne his last letter to his sister, as he was unable to see her to say goodbye. Haslam was ready to go with Keats to Italy, but circumstances made this impossible, and he took upon himself instead to arrange for Severn to go. Keats saw Fanny Brawne for the last time on 13 September. He could not bring himself thereafter to write to her, or read her letters. Keats raised cash by assigning his copyrights to Taylor & Hessey, assisted by Haslam and Woodhouse. This was the closest he came to making a will. He boarded the *Mary Crowther* in London Docks on 17 September with Severn and sailed to Gravesend, accompanied by the faithful Haslam.

Keats and Severn parted with Haslam and sailed from Gravesend on the night of 18 September. They were repeatedly delayed, first by storms, then by calms. On 28 September they landed at Portsmouth and visited the Snooks at Bedhampton. After further false starts the voyage finally began around 2 October. It proved a dreadful ordeal. Keats repeatedly coughed until he spat blood. He sank into a deep depression. Severn was astonished at his survival. They reached Naples on 21 October but were held in quarantine for ten days, Keats's condition constantly deteriorating. In spite of this he forced himself to the appearance of gaiety, summoning up puns for Severn and somehow finding the strength to write to Mrs Brawne. 31 October was Keats's twenty-fifth birthday. Passport formalities were not completed until well into November, and he did not reach Rome until 15 November. They took lodgings on the Piazza di Spagna, living on money cashed from his publishers' draft. Keats's last known letter, written to Brown on 30 November, speaks of his 'habitual feeling of my real life having past, and that I am leading a posthumous existence'. It ends 'I can scarcely bid you good bye even in a letter. I always made an awkward bow' (*L*. ii. 359). The final relapse came on 10 December. After much suffering, borne sometimes with great courage and fortitude, and sometimes with a terrible railing against his fate, Keats died at 11 p.m. on 23 February 1821. He was buried three days later in the Protestant Cemetery in Rome. Severn, who cared for him faithfully to the last, carried out his request that his gravestone be inscribed 'Here lies one whose name was writ in water'.

Notes

CHAPTER 1. WHY READ KEATS

1. G. M. Matthews (ed.), *Keats: The Critical Heritage* (London: Routledge, 1971), 35.
2. See e.g. Marjorie Levinson, *Keats's Life of Allegory: The Origins of a Style* (Oxford: Blackwell, 1988), and Jerome J. McGann, 'Keats and the Historical Method in Literary Criticism', *MLN* 94 (1979).

CHAPTER 2. OCTOBER 1795–OCTOBER 1816: EARLY POEMS

1. Leigh Hunt, *Lord Byron and Some of his Contemporaries* (London: Henry Colburn, 1828), 247.
2. Charles Cowden Clarke, *Recollections of Writers* (London: Sampson Low & Co., 1878), 123.
3. *The Keats Circle*, ed. Hyder E. Rollins, 2 vols., 2nd edn. (Cambridge, Mass.: Harvard University Press, 1965), ii. 163–5.
4. Richard Monckton Milnes, *Life, Letters, and Literary Remains of John Keats*, 2 vols. (London: Edward Moxon, 1848), i. 13.
5. Clarke, *Recollections*, 124.
6. Milnes, *Life*, i. 12.
7. *Keats Circle*, ed. Rollins, ii. 186.

CHAPTER 3. OCTOBER 1816–APRIL 1818: 'I STOOD TIP-TOE...', 'SLEEP AND POETRY', *ENDYMION*

1. Leigh Hunt, *Lord Byron and Some of his Contemporaries* (London: Henry Colburn, 1828), 249.
2. Charles Cowden Clarke, *Recollections of Writers* (London: Sampson Low & Co., 1878), 138.
3. Ibid. 140.

4. *Athenaeum*, 7 June 1873, 725.
5. *Woodhouse Poetry Transcripts,* ed. Jack Stillinger (New York: Garland, 1988), 4.
6. *Diaries of Benjamin Robert Haydon*, ed. Willard Pope, 5 vols. (Cambridge, Mass.: Harvard University Press, 1960–3), ii. 316.
7. *Woodhouse's Annotated Copy of Poems (1817)*, ed. Jack Stillinger (New York: Garland, 1985), 153.
8. *The Keats Circle*, ed. Hyder E. Rollins, 2 vols. 2nd edn. (Cambridge, Mass.: Harvard University Press, 1965), ii. 144.

CHAPTER 4. APRIL–MAY 1818: *ISABELLA*

1. E. P. Thompson, *William Morris: Romantic to Revolutionary* (London: Merlin Press, 1977), 11.
2. John Kerrigan, 'Writing Numbers: Keats, Hopkins, and the History of Chance', in Nicholas Roe (ed.), *Keats and History* (Cambridge: Cambridge University Press, 1995), 280–308, 287.

CHAPTER 5. MAY 1818–APRIL 1810: *THE EVE OF ST AGNES, HYPERION*

1. *Blackwood's Edinburgh Magazine*, 3 (Aug. 1818), 524.
2. *British Critic*, NS 9 (June 1818), 649–54.
3. Quoted in *John Keats: The Complete Poems*, ed. John Barnard, 3rd edn. (Harmondsworth: Penguin, 1988), 646–7.
4. See Christopher Ricks, *Keats and Embarrassment* (Oxford: Oxford University Press, 1974).

CHAPTER 6. APRIL–MAY 1819: THE ODES

1. *The Keats Circle*, ed. Hyder E. Rollins, 2 vols. 2nd edn. (Cambridge, Mass.: Harvard University Press, 1965), ii. 65.

CHAPTER 7. JUNE 1819–FEBRUARY 1821: *LAMIA*, 'TO AUTUMN', *THE FALL OF HYPERION*

1. William Sharp, *The Life and Letters of Joseph Severn* (London: Sampson Low & Co., 1892), 41.
2. *The Keats Circle*, ed. Hyder E. Rollins, 2 vols., 2nd edn. (Cambridge,

Mass.: Harvard University Press, 1965). ii. 73–4.

3. *Maria Gisborne & Edward Williams: Their Journals and Letters*, ed. F. Jones (Norman, Okla.: University of Oklahoma Press, 1951), 40.

Select Bibliography

EDITIONS OF KEATS'S WRITINGS

The Letters of John Keats, ed. Hyder E. Rollins, 2 vols. (Cambridge, Mass.: Harvard University Press, 1958). The standard complete edition of Keats's letters, completed to a very high standard of accuracy, and with a wealth of informative contextual material.

Letters of John Keats, ed. Robert Gittings (Oxford: Oxford University Press, 1970). The best selection, including all of the important letters.

The Poems of John Keats, ed. Miriam Allott (London: Longman, 1970). Contains very full and interesting annotation.

The Poems of John Keats, ed. Jack Stillinger (Cambridge, Mass.: Harvard University Press, 1978). The standard complete modern edition.

John Keats: The Complete Poems, ed. John Barnard, 3rd edn. (Harmondsworth: Penguin, 1988). The best compact reading text, thoughtful, scholarly, and with helpful detailed notes.

John Keats, ed. Elizabeth Cook (Oxford: Oxford University Press, 1990). Useful in including a generous selection from the letters, together with Keats's most notable prose writings.

John Keats: Selected Poems, ed. Nicholas Roe (London: Dent, 1995). Good selection with informative notes and other contextual material.

BIOGRAPHIES

The Keats Circle, ed. Hyder E. Rollins, 2 vols., 2nd edn. (Cambridge, Mass.: Harvard University Press, 1965). Includes the contents of the major collection of Keats material at Harvard; a fascinating and absolutely indispensable source of biographical and contextual information.

Bate, W. J., *John Keats* (Cambridge, Mass.: Harvard University Press, 1963). A monumental study, exhaustive and minutely detailed in following Keats's life and intellectual development. Not easy to use as a reference source, but immensely illuminating on Keats's personality and artistic achievement.

Gittings, Robert, *John Keats* (London: Heinemann, 1968). The most thoroughly researched and factually reliable of all biographies, persuasively inward with Keats's milieu and circumstances, particularly in early life. Some challenging and controversial conclusions.

Motion, Andrew, *Keats* (London: Faber, 1997). Very thorough, thoughtful, and critically engaged biography, emphasizing the political and cultural contexts. Absorbing in its careful extended passages of detailed critical reading.

Wallace, Jennifer (ed.), *Lives of the Great Romantics: Keats* (London: Pickering & Chatto, 1997). Serviceable and informative selection of documents from the earlier biographical tradition.

Ward, Aileen, *John Keats: The Making of a Poet* (London: Secker & Warburg, 1963). Very readable and well-researched biography, particularly good on the public context and with thoughtful reflection on Keats's psychological development.

CRITICAL STUDIES

Arnold, Matthew, 'John Keats', in *Essays in Criticism: Second Series* (London: Macmillan, 1888). A seminal essay (first published in 1880), definitively establishing Keats amongst the major English poets.

Aske, Martin, *Keats and Hellenism* (Cambridge: Cambridge University Press, 1985). Establishes a context for close reading of the poetry in Keats's engagement with the problem of the representation of antiquity.

Barnard, John, *John Keats* (Cambridge: Cambridge University Press, 1987). Excellent broad introductory discussion.

Bayley, John, *The Uses of Division* (London: Chatto & Windus, 1976). Includes an influential essay on Keats's style.

Bennett, Andrew, *Keats, Narrative and Audience: The Posthumous Life of Writing* (Cambridge: Cambridge University Press, 1994). Witty, lively, entertaining, but also sometimes abstract and difficult study; a stimulating and original discussion informed by recent theory.

Blackstone, Bernard, *The Consecrated Urn* (London: Longman, 1959). Idiosyncratic study, mixing insightful originality with an eccentric reliance on highly debatable intellectual contexts (such as Platonism).

Bloom, Harold, *The Visionary Company,* rev. edn. (Ithaca, N: Cornell

University Press, 1971). An immensely influential study, offering a powerful argument about English Romantic poetry, which includes a searching chapter on Keats's poetic development.

—— (ed.), *The Odes of Keats* (New York: Chelsea House, 1987).

Brooks, Cleanth, *The Well Wrought Urn* (New York, 1947). Includes a famous 'new critical' reading of the 'Ode on a Grecian Urn'.

Butler, Marilyn, *Romantics, Rebels and Reactionaries* (Oxford: Oxford University Press, 1981). Important contextual study of British Romantic culture, setting Keats in highly original and suggestive new perspectives.

de Almeida, Hermione (ed.), *Critical Essays on John Keats* (Boston: Hall, 1990).

—— *Romantic Medicine and John Keats* (New York: Oxford University Press, 1991). Very well-researched and thoughtful discussion of Keats and medicine.

Dickstein, Morris, *Keats and his Poetry: A Study in Development* (Chicago: University of Chicago Press, 1971). A reading of Keats's development in terms of his changing attitudes to 'consciousness'.

Ende, Stuart A., *Keats and the Sublime* (New Haven: Yale University Press, 1976).

Evert, Walter, *Aesthetic and Myth in the Poetry of Keats* (Princeton: Princeton University Press, 1965).

Finney, Claude Lee, *The Evolution of Keats's Poetry*, 2 vols. (Cambridge, Mass.: Harvard University Press, 1936). A massive compilation of basic information on Keats's poems, still useful.

Fraser, G. S. (ed.), *John Keats: Odes* (Casebook; London: Macmillan, 1971).

Goellnicht, Donald C., *The Poet-Physician: Keats and Medical Science* (Pittsburgh: University of Pittsburgh Press, 1984). Intelligent commentary on Keats's poetry in the light of his medical knowledge.

Jack, Ian, *Keats and the Mirror of Art* (Oxford: Oxford University Press, 1967). Informative discussion of the influence of the visual arts in Keats's work.

Jones, John, *John Keats's Dream of Truth* (1969). A quirky but very interesting book on Keats's style, much influenced by Bayley (see above).

Kitson, Peter (ed.), *Coleridge, Keats and Shelley* (New Casebook; London: Macmillan, 1996).

Kucich, Greg, *Keats, Shelley, and Romantic Spenserianism* (University Park, Pa.: Pennsylvania State University Press, 1991).

Levinson, Marjorie, *Keats's Life of Allegory: The Origins of a Style* (Oxford: Blackwell, 1988). A challenging and controversial reading, which has occasioned fierce debate. It considers Keats in a historical light,

116

deeply informed by recent theory, and coloured by original but also deeply debatable contention.

McGann, Jerome J., *The Beauty of Inflections: Literary Investigations in Historical Method and Theory* (Oxford: Clarendon Press, 1985). Includes an important essay on Keats and History.

Matthews G. M. (ed.), *Keats: The Critical Heritage* (London: Routledge, 1971). Excellent documentary history of Keats's reception and early reputation, with an important introductory essay.

Mayhead, Robin, *John Keats* (Cambridge: Cambridge University Press, 1967). Useful introductory study.

Middleton Murry, J., *Keats and Shakespeare* (Oxford: Oxford University Press, 1925). A very influential study.

—— *Keats* (London: Jonathan Cape, 1955). Subsumes and revises earlier studies by Murry; now old-fashioned and eccentric, but still offers numerous insights.

Muir, Kenneth (ed.), *John Keats: A Reassessment* (Liverpool: Liverpool University Press, 1958). Very good critical essays by various hands, including an influential essay on the two Hyperion poems by Muir.

Patterson, Charles I., *The Daemonic in the Poetry of Keats* (Urbana, Ill.: University of Illinois Press, 1970). An interestingly distinctive study, which challenges familiar frames of reference.

Perkins, David, *The Quest for Permanence: The Symbolism of Wordsworth, Shelley, and Keats* (Cambridge, Mass.: Harvard University Press, 1959). Keats is central in the argument of this powerful book, which considers problems of time and mortality in Romantic poetry.

Pettet, E. C., *On the Poetry of John Keats* (Cambridge: Cambridge University Press, 1957). A mixed bag, but with some illuminating passages.

Ricks, Christopher, *Keats and Embarrassment* (Oxford: Oxford University Press, 1976). A brilliantly original critical study, superb in its attention to the detailed workings of the poetry.

Ridley, M. R., *Keats's Craftsmanship: A Study in Poetic Development* (Oxford: Oxford University Press, 1933). A detailed study of Keats's methods of composition, using the manuscript collection at Harvard.

Roe, Nicholas (ed.), *Keats and History* (Cambridge: Cambridge University Press, 1995). A very good collection of essays by a range of leading British and American Romanticists.

—— *John Keats and the Culture of Dissent* (Oxford: Clarendon Press, 1997). Interesting and suggestive discussion of the cultural context.

Ryan, Robert M., *Keats: The Religious Sense* (Princeton: Princeton University Press, 1976). A very carefully researched investigation of Keats's 'religious milieu'.

—— and Sharp, Ronald A. (eds), *The Persistence of Poetry: Bicentennial*

117

Essays on Keats (Amherst, Mass.: University of Massachusetts Press, 1998).

Scott, Grant F., *The Sculpted Word: Keats, Ekphrasis and the Visual Arts* (Hanover: University Press of New England, 1994).

Sharp, Ronald A., *Keats, Scepticism, and the Religion of Beauty* (Athens, Ga.: University of Georgia Press, 1979).

Slote, Bernice, *Keats and the Dramatic Principle* (Lincoln, Neb.: University of Nebraska Press, 1958). A very interesting study, based in Keats's interest in the theatre, but ranging widely.

Sperry, Stuart M., *Keats the Poet* (Princeton: Princeton University Press, 1973). Probably the best critical study of Keats's poetry; essential reading.

Spurgeon, Caroline, *Keats's Shakespeare: A Descriptive Study* (Oxford: Clarendon Press, 1928). Highly informative.

Stillinger, Jack (ed.), *Twentieth Century Interpretations of Keats's Odes: A Collection of Critical Essays* (Englewood Cliffs, NJ: Prentice-Hall, 1968).

—— *The Hoodwinking of Madeline and Other Essays* (Urbana, Ill.: University of Illinois Press, 1971). Important collection of essays by one of Keats's most distinguished modern scholar-critics.

—— *The Texts of Keats's Poems* (Cambridge, Mass.: Harvard University Press, 1974). An authoritative scholarly commentary on the editorial work embodied in Stillinger's edition of the poems (see above).

Thorpe, Clarence D., *The Mind of John Keats* (Oxford: Oxford University Press, 1926). Immensely influential study in its time.

Trilling, Lionel, *The Opposing Self* (London: Secker & Warburg, 1955). Includes a famous essay on Keats.

Vendler, Helen, *The Odes of John Keats* (Cambridge, Mass.: Harvard University Press, 1983). Fine and demanding critical study.

Wasserman, Earl R., *The Finer Tone: Keats's Major Poems* (Baltimore: Johns Hopkins Press, 1953). A challenging and densely argued study, sometimes difficult, but rewarding.

Watkins, Daniel P., *Keats's Poetry and the Politics of the Imagination* (Rutherford, NJ: Fairleigh Dickinson University Press, 1989). A 'new historicist' study.

Wolfson, Susan J. (ed.), 'Keats and Politics: A Forum', *Studies in Romanticism*, 25 (1986). Excellent collection of new essays by leading critics.

—— *The Questioning Presence: Wordsworth, Keats, and the Interrogative Mode in Romantic Poetry* (Ithaca, NY: Cornell University Press, 1986). Particularly interesting on Wordsworth's influence on Keats.

—— (ed.), *The Cambridge Companion to John Keats* (Cambridge: Cambridge University Press, 2001).

Index

Recent and Forthcoming Titles in the New Series of

WRITERS AND THEIR WORK

WRITERS AND THEIR WORK

RECENT & FORTHCOMING TITLES

Title	Author
Peter Ackroyd	Susana Onega
Kingsley Amis	Richard Bradford
Anglo-Saxon Verse	Graham Holderness
Antony and Cleopatra 2/e	Ken Parker
As You Like It	Penny Gay
W. H. Auden	Stan Smith
Jane Austen	Robert Miles
Alan Ayckbourn	Michael Holt
J. G. Ballard	Michel Delville
Pat Barker	Sharon Monteith
Djuna Barnes	Deborah Parsons
Julian Barnes	Matthew Pateman
Aphra Behn 2/e	Sue Wiseman
John Betjeman	Dennis Brown
Edward Bond	Michael Mangan
Anne Brontë	Betty Jay
Emily Brontë	Stevie Davies
A. S. Byatt	Richard Todd
Byron	Drummond Bone
Caroline Drama	Julie Sanders
Angela Carter	Lorna Sage
Geoffrey Chaucer	Steve Ellis
Children's Literature	Kimberley Reynolds
Caryl Churchill 2/e	Elaine Aston
John Clare	John Lucas
S. T. Coleridge	Stephen Bygrave
Joseph Conrad	Cedric Watts
Crime Fiction	Martin Priestman
Shashi Deshpande	Armrita Bhalla
Charles Dickens	Rod Mengham
John Donne	Stevie Davies
Carol Ann Duffy 2/e	Deryn Rees Jones
Early Modern Sonneteers	Michael Spiller
George Eliot	Josephine McDonagh
English Translators of Homer	Simeon Underwood
Henry Fielding	Jenny Uglow
Veronica Forrest-Thomson – Language Poetry	Alison Mark
E. M. Forster	Nicholas Royle
John Fowles	William Stephenson
Athol Fugard	Dennis Walder
Elizabeth Gaskell	Kate Flint
The Gawain-Poet	John Burrow
The Georgian Poets	Rennie Parker
William Golding	Kevin McCarron
Graham Greene	Peter Mudford
Neil Gunn	J. B. Pick
Ivor Gurney	John Lucas
Hamlet 2/e	Ann Thompson & Neil Taylor
Thomas Hardy	Peter Widdowson
David Hare	Jeremy Ridgman
Tony Harrison	Joe Kelleher

RECENT & FORTHCOMING TITLES

Title	Author
William Hazlitt	J. B. Priestley; R. L. Brett (intro. by Michael Foot)
Seamus Heaney 2/e	Andrew Murphy
George Herbert	T.S. Eliot (intro. by Peter Porter)
Geoffrey Hill	Andrew Roberts
Gerard Manley Hopkins	Daniel Brown
Henrik Ibsen	Sally Ledger
Kazuo Ishiguro	Cynthia Wong
Henry James – The Later Writing	Barbara Hardy
James Joyce	Steven Connor
Julius Caesar	Mary Hamer
Franz Kafka	Michael Wood
John Keats	Kelvin Everest
Hanif Kureishi	Ruvani Ranasinha
William Langland: Piers Plowman	Claire Marshall
King Lear	Terence Hawkes
Philip Larkin	Laurence Lerner
D. H. Lawrence	Linda Ruth Williams
Doris Lessing	Elizabeth Maslen
C. S. Lewis	William Gray
Wyndham Lewis	Andrzej Gasiorak
David Lodge	Bernard Bergonzi
Katherine Mansfield	Andrew Bennett
Christopher Marlowe	Thomas Healy
Andrew Marvell	Annabel Patterson
Ian McEwan	Kiernan Ryan
Measure for Measure	Kate Chedgzoy
A Midsummer Night's Dream	Helen Hackett
Alice Munro	Ailsa Cox
Vladimir Nabokov	Neil Cornwell
V. S. Naipaul	Suman Gupta
Edna O'Brien	Amanda Greenwood
Ben Okri	Robert Fraser
Walter Pater	Laurel Brake
Brian Patten	Linda Cookson
Harold Pinter	Mark Batty
Sylvia Plath 2/e	Elisabeth Bronfen
Jean Rhys	Helen Carr
Richard II	Margaret Healy
Richard III	Edward Burns
Dorothy Richardson	Carol Watts
John Wilmot, Earl of Rochester	Germaine Greer
Romeo and Juliet	Sasha Roberts
Christina Rossetti	Kathryn Burlinson
Salman Rushdie	Damian Grant
Paul Scott	Jacqueline Banerjee
The Sensation Novel	Lyn Pykett
P. B. Shelley	Paul Hamilton
Wole Soyinka	Mpalive Msiska
Muriel Spark	Brian Cheyette
Edmund Spenser	Colin Burrow
Laurence Sterne	Manfred Pfister
D. M. Thomas	Bran Nicol
Dylan Thomas	Chris Wiggington

RECENT & FORTHCOMING TITLES

Title	Author
J. R. R. Tolkien	*Charles Moseley*
Leo Tolstoy	*John Bayley*
Charles Tomlinson	*Tim Clark*
Anthony Trollope	*Andrew Sanders*
Victorian Quest Romance	*Robert Fraser*
Edith Wharton	*Janet Beer*
Angus Wilson	*Peter Conradi*
Mary Wollstonecraft	*Jane Moore*
Women's Gothic 2/e	*Emma Clery*
Virginia Woolf 2/e	*Laura Marcus*
Working Class Fiction	*Ian Haywood*
W. B. Yeats	*Edward Larrissy*
Charlotte Yonge	*Alethea Hayter*

TITLES IN PREPARATION

Title	Author
Chinua Achebe	*Nahem Yousaf*
Fleur Adcock	*Janet Wilson*
Ama Ata Aidoo	*Nana Wilson-Tagoe*
Matthew Arnold	*Kate Campbell*
Margaret Atwood	*Marion Wynne-Davies*
John Banville	*Peter Dempsey*
Black British Fiction	*Mark Stein*
William Blake	*Steven Vine*
Elizabeth Bowen	*Maud Ellmann*
Charlotte Brontë	*Margaret Reynolds*
Robert Browning	*John Woodford*
John Bunyan	*Tamsin Spargoe*
Bruce Chatwin	*Kerry Featherstone*
Cymbeline	*Peter Swaab*
Anita Desai	*Elaine Ho*
Margaret Drabble	*Glenda Leeming*
John Dryden	*David Hopkins*
T. S. Eliot	*Colin MacCabe*
J. G. Farrell	*John McLeod*
Brian Friel	*Geraldine Higgins*
Nadine Gordimer	*Lewis Nkosi*
Geoffrey Grigson	*R. M. Healey*
Ted Hughes	*Susan Bassnett*
Samuel Johnson	*Liz Bellamy*
Ben Jonson	*Anthony Johnson*
James Kelman	*Gustav Klaus*
Jack Kerouac	*Michael Hrebebiak*
Jamaica Kincaid	*Susheila Nasta*
Rudyard Kipling	*Jan Montefiore*
Charles and Mary Lamb	*Michael Baron*
Roamond Lehmann	*Judy Simon*
Una Marson & Louise Bennett	*Alison Donnell*
Merchant of Venice	*Warren Chernaik*
John Milton	*Jonathan Sawday*
Bharati Mukherjee	*Manju Sampat*
R. K. Narayan	*Shirley Chew*
New Women Writers	*Marion Shaw*
Grace Nichols	*Sarah Lawson-Welsh*
Caryl Phillips	*Helen Thomas*
Religious Poets of the 17th Century	*Helen Wilcox*
Revenge Tragedy	*Janet Clare*
Samuel Richardson	*David Deeming*
Nayantara Sahgal	*Ranjana Ash*
Sam Selvon	*Ramchand & Salick*
Sir Walter Scott	*Harriet Harvey-Wood*
Mary Shelley	*Catherine Sharrock*
Charlotte Smith & Helen Williams	*Angela Keane*
Christopher Smart	*Neil Curry*
Stevie Smith	*Martin Gray*
R. L. Stevenson	*David Robb*
Gertrude Stein	*Nicola Shaughnessy*
Bram Stoker	*Andrew Maunder*
Tom Stoppard	*Nicholas Cadden*

TITLES IN PREPARATION

Title	Author
Graham Swift	*Peter Widdowson*
Jonathan Swift	*Ian Higgins*
Algernon Swinburne	*Catherine Maxwell*
Tennyson	*Seamus Perry*
W. M. Thackeray	*Richard Salmon*
Three Avant-Garde Poets	*Peter Middleton*
Derek Walcott	*Stephen Regan*
Marina Warner	*Laurence Coupe*
Jeanette Winterson	*Angela Leighton*
Women Romantic Poets	*Anne Janowitz*
Women Writers of the 17th Century	*Ramona Wray*